# Buddha Jumps Over the Wall,

## and Other Curiously Named Classic Chinese Dishes

# Buddha Jumps Over the Wall,

## and Other Curiously Named Classic Chinese Dishes

**YING CHANG COMPESTINE**
Illustrations by **Vivian Truong**

ES * A GRAPHIC COOKBOOK * 26 REC

ES & STORIES * A GRAPHIC COOKBO

Library of Congress Cataloging-in-Publication Data

Names: Compestine, Ying Chang, author. | Truong, Vivian,
    illustrator.
Title: Buddha jumps over the wall, : and other curiously
    named classic Chinese dishes / Ying Chang Compestine ;
    illustrations by Vivian Truong.
Description: San Francisco : Chronicle Books, [2025] |
    Includes index.
Identifiers: LCCN 2024038044 | ISBN 9781797218267
    (paperback)
Subjects: LCSH: Cooking, Chinese. | LCGFT: Cookbooks.
Classification: LCC TX724.5.C5 C649 2025 | DDC
    641.5951--dc23/eng/20240907
LC record available at https://lccn.loc.gov/2024038044

Manufactured in India.

FSC™
MIX
Paper | Supporting
responsible forestry
FSC™ C043100
www.fsc.org

Design by Vanessa Dina.
Typesetting by Wynne Au-Yeung.

10 9 8 7 6 5 4 3 2 1

Chronicle books and gifts are available at special quantity
discounts to corporations, professional associations, literacy
programs, and other organizations. For details and discount
information, please contact our premiums department at
corporatesales@chroniclebooks.com or at 1-800-759-0190.

Chronicle Books LLC
680 Second Street
San Francisco, California 94107
www.chroniclebooks.com

# Contents

## Chapter 3
# Desserts (甜點) **138**

# Prologue

Growing up in Wuhan, China, I always had to outsmart my two older brothers when it came to food. I realized that scuffling with them at the dinner table was a lost cause—the best strategy was to go straight to the source. I would follow Nai Nai, my grandmother, into the kitchen and huddle around the steamer like a puppy, begging for leftovers.

Nai Nai let me sample every dish she cooked. "Try some ants climbing a tree." She would wrap the noodles around the tip of her chopsticks like a drumstick and give it to me. Or she would say, "Oh, the ignored by doggy buns are ready! They taste best when they're warm." She would put the meat buns on a plate.

"Why such strange names, Nai Nai?" I'd ask between bites.

As she diced tofu and carved bamboo shoots into miniature trees, green onions into brushes, tomatoes into roses, and carrots and icicle radishes into flowers, Nai Nai would tell me the tales.

At dinnertime, with a mischievous look, I would ask my brothers, "Are you going to eat some ants? Do you want to eat the buns that even the dog doesn't want?"

"Ants?!" they'd shout. As their chopsticks froze in the air and they looked at each other in disgust, I would fill my bowl.

I would burst with pride when reciting to them the stories Nai Nai told me. We savored the delicious noodles, covered with flavorful minced pork, and buns stuffed with juicy meat and chive fillings.

As I got older, I would help Nai Nai stretch noodles and roll meatballs while she told me the story behind each dish. Those were some of the happiest moments of my childhood.

Many years later, I found myself retelling these same stories to my own little kitchen helper—my young son, Vinson. When we served these dishes to guests, he would call out the names of the dishes and wait for their reactions with a naughty smile.

"Beggar's chicken, lion's head meatballs, Buddha jumps over the wall . . . "

The guests would ask, "Why such strange names?"

That question has led me to write this book for those who have an appetite for Chinese food and history and want to hear the stories of these strangely named, yet delicious, dishes.

# Introduction

Have you ever wondered where the names of some Chinese dishes come from? Why it's Ants Climbing a Tree (page 99) or Mapo Tofu (page 77), which means "bean curd made by a pockmarked old woman"? Then there's Goubuli Baozi (page 66), which literally translates to "ignored by doggy buns." You may think that if even a dog wouldn't eat them, then those must be some pretty awful buns. On the contrary—they are a much sought-after delicacy from Tianjin, a city in northern China.

Chinese culture places much importance on food, so dishes are often connected to a classic legend, a famous person, or a historical event. Storytelling is one of the most universal and collaborative components every culture has, from cautionary fairy tales spanning the Eastern and Western hemispheres, to folk stories shared amongst a community, passed from generation to generation. The subtitle of this book acknowledges that these recipes are "curious," but they are not odd to me, nor to the Chinese people who have relished these dishes since their childhood.

My own palate has been shaped extensively by my experience as a Chinese immigrant living in America. Working as a food editor for Martha Stewart *Body + Soul* magazine, I often had to inform my English-speaking peers about what Shaoxing wine, hoisin sauce, and star anise were, or explain the meaning behind these names. When hosting a dinner party, friends would curiously ask what "husband and wife lung slices" meant. To their delight, I would recite the story of an ancient couple who marinated beef lung so well, they disguised the fact that it was not a premium cut (page 18).

I have chosen to embrace the "strangeness" of these names to those outside of Chinese culture. I view these conversations as opportunities to humorously share Chinese culture with people who may not know of China's fascinating culinary history. After telling each story, I noticed the meat tasted fresher, the smell in the air was more pungent, and my guests were more excited in sharing their approval. It was then that I realized the power of storytelling. As Claudia Roden wrote, "Every cuisine tells a story."

In *Buddha Jumps Over the Wall, and Other Curiously Named Classic Chinese Dishes*, I explore the mystique that surrounds these dishes' origins and the reasons behind their unique names, along with their recipes. You may be familiar with some, while others can only be found in authentic Chinese restaurants. I have simplified the cooking steps of the book's 26 recipes, making them accessible by using easy-to-obtain ingredients. For example, traditional Beggar's Chicken (page 45) calls for a whole chicken, but I offer an option of using chicken breasts. In Ignored by Doggy Buns (page 66), I offer an option to use canned biscuit dough. With the simple shopping list I provide, you can easily obtain all the ingredients you need for these recipes from your local grocery or health food store.

The book also reveals the etiquette of Chinese dining, such as how to use chopsticks (page 172), how to eat from a rice bowl (page 177), and the proper way to drink tea (page 176). So when enjoying your next Chinese meal, you can show off your refined Chinese manners while telling your friends the stories behind the dishes. Hopefully they will bring the warmth and joy of my kitchen into yours!

# A Note about Ingredients

Glass noodles (粉丝), also called cellophane noodles, are round, thin noodles made from water and starch of mung bean or sweet potato. Once soaked in hot water, they become soft, pliable, and semi-transparent with a springy, slippery texture. After cooking, they become fully transparent. They have a plain taste but easily absorb flavor when mixed with seasonings and sauces.

Chili oil (or chili pepper oil, 辣椒油) is a red condiment made from vegetable oil, soybean oil, or sesame oil infused with chiles, five-spice powder, toasted sesame seeds, ground Sichuan peppercorns, whole star anise, and bay leaves. It has a fragrant, spicy, nutty taste.

Doubanjiang (豆瓣酱), also known as spicy fermented bean sauce or broad bean sauce, is one of the key ingredients in Sichuan cuisine. It has a strong, fermented taste that is simultaneously savory, salty, and spicy. The best broad bean sauce is made in Pixian, a small county in Sichuan province. You can buy doubanjiang in Asian grocery stores and online.

Dried lotus leaves (干粽叶) are first soaked in warm water until soft and then used to wrap various foods or line steamers. While cooking, the leaves release an exotic perfume and impart a mild, sweet flavor to the dish. You can find dried lotus leaves in Asian markets and online; you can also substitute banana or grape leaves for them.

Fermented red chili bean curd (紅腐乳), also known as fermented tofu, is made from tofu fermented in a mixture of anise, cinnamon, dried baby shrimp, rice wine, and sugar. It has a distinctly thick, creamy texture and a strong, acrid smell. It's a common ingredient used in many Chinese dishes.

Fish sauce (鱼露) is an amber-colored liquid made from the fermentation of fish or shrimp with sea salt. It is used in marinades, stir-fries, and dipping sauces. Its briny, salty flavor brings out the savory taste of many dishes.

**Glutinous rice (糯米)**, also known as sweet or sticky rice, is a variety of short-grain rice with a round, pearl-like form. High in starch, it turns translucent when cooked, and the texture is soft and sticky. It is widely used in Asian desserts and festival dishes.

**Hoisin sauce (海鲜酱)** is a thick, salty-sweet sauce typically used in many Cantonese dishes as a glaze or for dipping. It usually consists of garlic, fermented soybeans, red chiles, and other ingredients, depending on the region where it is made. If you don't have hoisin sauce on hand, you can replace it with bean paste, miso paste with extra soy sauce, oyster sauce, or fish sauce.

**Oyster sauce (蚝油)** is a dark-colored sauce made from oyster extracts, sugar, salt, and soy sauce. It's commonly used in many Asian stir-fry dishes as a topping or dipping sauce. It brings out the savory umami flavor of foods, especially in seafood and vegetable dishes.

**Rock sugar (冰糖)** is a solid, see-through sugar crystal that resembles tiny ice lumps. It is formed from boiled sugar syrup that cools into rock-like crystals over a few days. While less sweet than regular sugar, its honey-like taste is used to balance salty or sour dishes. It also creates an enticing gleam when used in braised dishes. Many cooks in China add rock sugar to tea for a mild sweetness. You can find rock sugar at Asian grocers and online.

**Sichuan peppercorn (花椒)**, like doubanjiang, is another key ingredient in Sichuan cuisine. It lends a distinct, irreplaceable aroma, citrusy taste, and mouth-numbing, tingling sensation. You can buy Sichuan peppercorns, whole or powdered, at Asian grocery stores and online.

**Star anise (八角)** is derived from the fruit that grows on the *Illicium verum* plant, which is native to Southwest China. The points of the fruit's star-shaped pod contain a pea-size seed. Both the seeds and pods have a sweet, licorice-like flavor. Star anise is a key ingredient in five-spice powder (along with cloves, cinnamon, fennel, and Sichuan peppercorns).

Chapter 1

# Appet
# (開胃菜

izers

# HUSBAND AND WIFE LUNG SLICES

During the Qing dynasty (1644-1911), in the city of Chengdu, there lived a married couple: Guo Zhaohua and Zhang Tianzheng.

Every day they worked tirelessly together in a street stall, selling thinly sliced, cheap beef offal with homemade spicy sauce. Only poor people-rickshaw pullers, farmers, street vendors-ate their food.

One day, a mischievous boy pulled a prank on the couple. He stuck paper notes that read "fu qi fei pian" ("husband and wife selling wasted slices") on their backs.

The customers laughed and cheered, and started calling their dish fu qi fei pian. The couple ended up adopting the name.

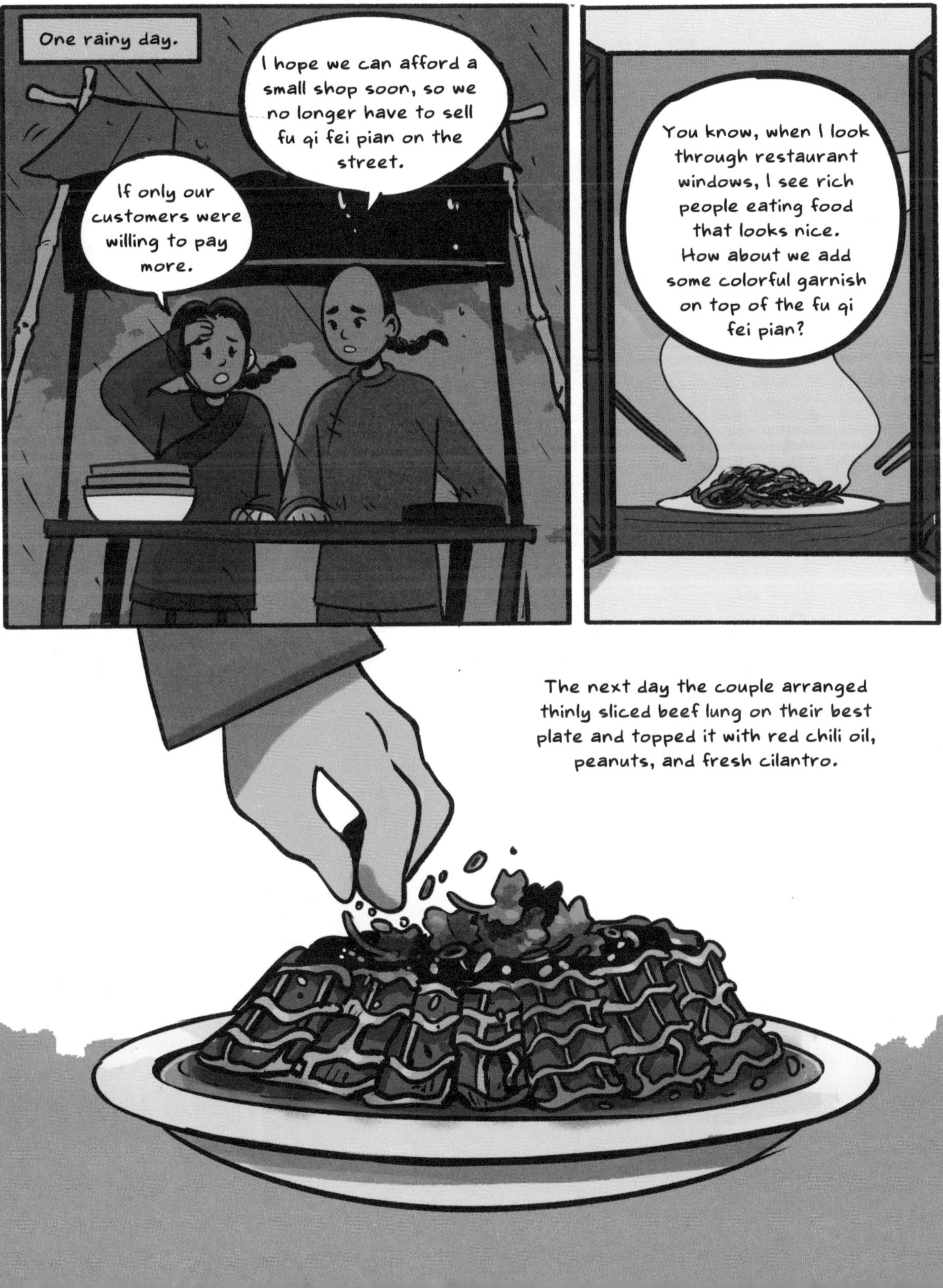
One rainy day.
I hope we can afford a small shop soon, so we no longer have to sell fu qi fei pian on the street.
If only our customers were willing to pay more.
You know, when I look through restaurant windows, I see rich people eating food that looks nice. How about we add some colorful garnish on top of the fu qi fei pian?
The next day the couple arranged thinly sliced beef lung on their best plate and topped it with red chili oil, peanuts, and fresh cilantro.

Soon after, a businessman dressed in an expensive silk robe stopped by their cart and placed an order.

Mmmm. This flavor is unique. What's in it?

It's . . .

It's beef lung, sir. It was the only fresh beef organ we could get today.

Well, I would have never eaten beef lung. But with your sauce, it tastes delicious!

The man dropped a silver coin and walked away.

Weeks later, when the businessman returned, the couple served him beef lung along with beef tendon.

The man enjoyed it so much that he came back with his friends, who then returned with their friends, and so on.

Months later, the couple had finally saved enough money to open a small restaurant.

On opening day, the businessman gifted them a gold-lettered plaque. He changed the character fei (廢), which originally meant waste, to lung (肺), as the two words have the same pronunciation, so the dish sounded more appetizing.

夫妻肺片

In time, fu qi fei pian became popular all over the world. Over the years, chefs have modified the dish. Today, people rarely use beef offal for it—they use beef and beef tendon instead. So next time you go to a restaurant and see fu qi fei pian on the menu, rest assured you are not eating anyone's lungs!

# HUSBAND AND WIFE LUNG SLICES
## （夫妻肺片）

---

Translated literally, *fu qi fei pian* means "husband and wife lung slices." Traditionally, this dish is served as a cold appetizer. The beef is braised in a savory broth, then thinly sliced and garnished with cilantro, toasted sesame seeds, and chopped peanuts. To save time, you can cook this in an Instant Pot or a pressure cooker.

### Makes 6 to 8 servings

3 to 3½ lb beef brisket

¼ cup plus 1 tsp soy sauce

¼ cup rice wine or dry sherry

1 Tbsp rock sugar or granulated sugar

4 dried chiles

3 green onions, cut into 4 in pieces

3 large slices fresh ginger

1 cinnamon stick

1 tsp whole Sichuan peppercorns plus 1 tsp toasted and ground

6 Tbsp sesame paste or tahini

¼ cup beef broth

¼ cup roughly chopped fresh cilantro

3 to 4 Tbsp chili oil

3 Tbsp chopped peanuts, toasted

2 Tbsp white sesame seeds, toasted

Chopped fresh cilantro, toasted sesame seeds, and chopped toasted peanuts, for garnishing

# HOW TO MAKE HUSBAND AND WIFE LUNG SLICES

Rinse the brisket under warm water.

Cut into big chunks.

Place it into a large stockpot and cover it completely with water, about 6 cups.

Bring to a boil over high heat, then reduce the heat to low and add the ¼ cup of the soy sauce, the rice wine, rock sugar, chiles, green onions, ginger, cinnamon, and the 1 tsp of whole peppercorns.

Simmer until fork-tender, 2 to 2½ hours.

Remove from the heat and allow the brisket to cool in the broth.

To make the sauce, in a medium bowl, combine the sesame paste, beef broth, cilantro, oil, peanuts, sesame seeds, the 1 tsp of ground peppercorns, and the remaining 1 tsp of soy sauce.

Set aside.

Once the beef is cool enough to handle, slice it against the grain into 1½ in pieces.

Arrange on a plate.

Drizzle with the sauce and garnish with the cilantro, sesame seeds, and peanuts.

Serve at room temperature or cold as an appetizer, or with rice or noodles as a main dish.

To store, seal leftovers in an airtight container and refrigerate for up to 5 days.

# THE STORY OF TEA

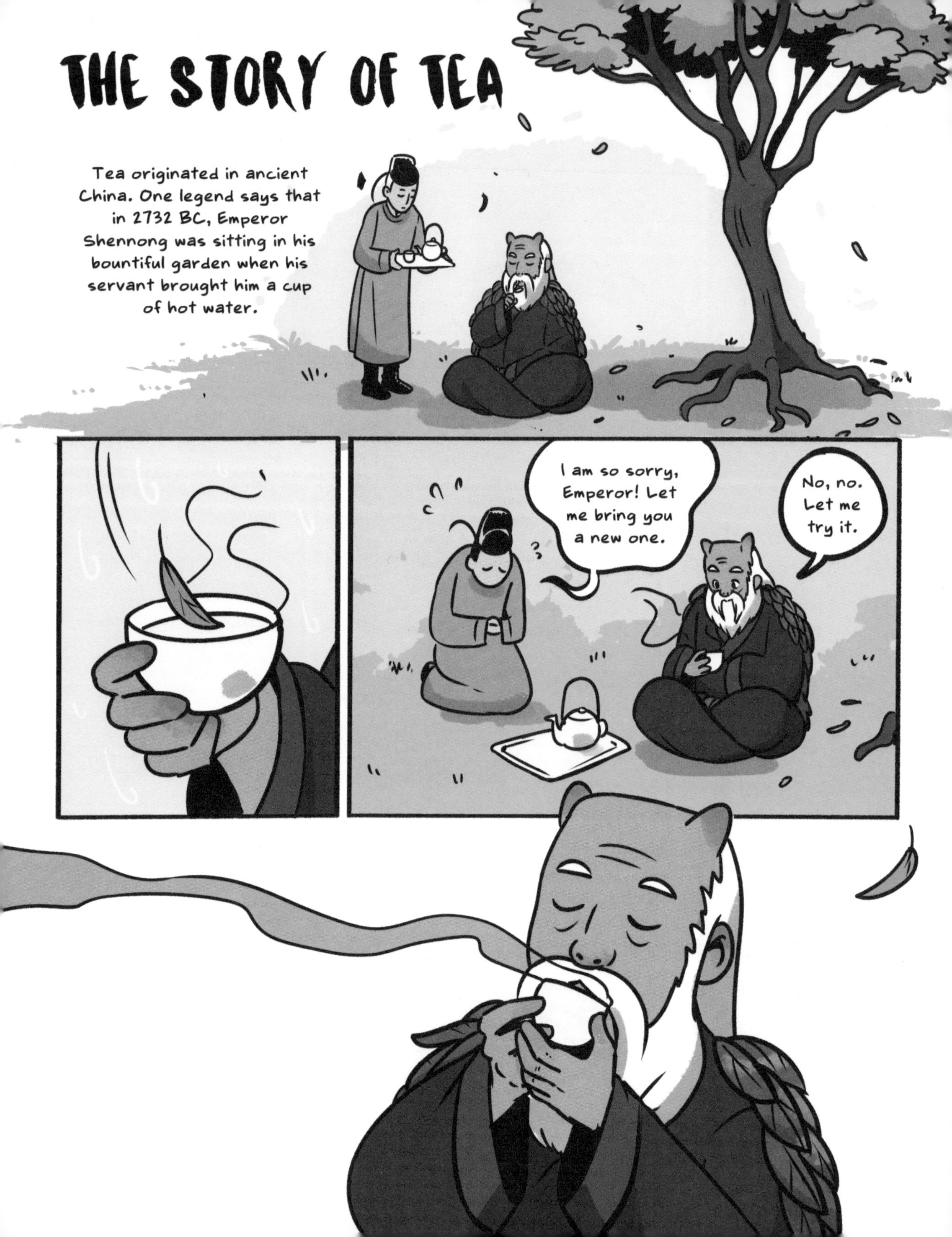
Tea originated in ancient China. One legend says that in 2732 BC, Emperor Shennong was sitting in his bountiful garden when his servant brought him a cup of hot water.
I am so sorry, Emperor! Let me bring you a new one.
No, no. Let me try it.

Mmm, I like it. Have a taste.

The servant took a sip. Instantly, the sweet and tangy flavor spread in his mouth, and fresh, warm liquid invigorated his body.

Wow, I have never tasted anything this good!

Me neither. Go pick some more leaves and make me another cup.

The next day, news of the emperor drinking water brewed with leaves spread throughout the imperial palace. A few of the emperor's mistresses tried it, and then his ministers and his generals. They all loved and raved about it to their families and servants.

The word of the tea spread rapidly. Townspeople rushed to rip leaves off trees and put them into their cups. Some brews soothed their bodies, while others tasted so bad they couldn't bring themselves to take a second sip. Eventually, folks learned which leaves produced what brews. For example, only leaves from *Camellia sinensis* trees emitted a delicate scent and had a fresh vegetable flavor when brewed in hot water.

I, too, developed my passion for tea by accident. One day, when I was about five years old, my father's best friend came for a visit.

This is the best tea from the new harvest, Enshi Yu Lu.

Father carefully put some tea leaves and hot water into two cups and covered them with small plates.

Why are you covering the cups, Daddy?

It allows the tea to cool slowly.

Wow, I've heard so much about it but never tried it! It smells so good! I can't wait to taste it.

He let me take my first sip. I was astounded by the fresh scent and bitter, minty taste.

Look. The tea leaves have sunk to the bottom. Tea is ready.

From then on, I loved to steal my father's tea from his cup while he was chatting with his friends.

I became a very skilled thief. By testing the cup with the back of my hand, I knew when the tea leaves had sunk to the bottom, and the tea was hot but not scalding.

I would open the cover and down the tea.

I then replaced the lid, and slipped the cup back where it belonged.

I enjoyed watching my father's look of surprise when he saw his empty teacup and exclaimed, "There is a hole in this cup!"

While he pretended to look for the hole, I would bring him hot water to refill the cup.

Because so many "holes" appeared in my father's cup, I received many teacups as birthday presents from his friends. But I never used them. I told people that you don't need your own teacup when you can use your father's.

Drinking tea now reminds me of the happiest moments I shared with my beloved father and my hometown, Wuhan.

# TEA EGGS

## （茶叶蛋）

In China, this is the most popular dish cooked with tea. Its flavor and color seep through the cracked shells into the tea eggs (also called marbled eggs), resulting in a stunning presentation. The longer the eggs soak in the sauce, the more flavorful they become. After you taste one, you may never want to eat plain hard-cooked eggs again. Marbled eggs are good as a garnish and ideal as a snack or lunch box filler.

**Makes 6 eggs**

6 large eggs
5 green tea bags
1 tsp freshly ground black pepper
One 1 in cinnamon stick
3 Tbsp low-sodium soy sauce
½ tsp five-spice powder
4 thin slices fresh ginger
2 dried red chiles (optional)

# HOW TO MAKE TEA EGGS

Place the eggs in a large saucepan.

Cover with cold water and bring to a boil over high heat. Reduce the heat to medium and cook the eggs for 7 minutes.

Remove the saucepan from the heat.

Using a spider or slotted spoon, lift the eggs out of the water one at a time.

Using the back of a large spoon, lightly tap the eggs over the entire shell to produce a spiderweb of cracks.

Do not peel the eggs.

Return the eggs to the saucepan.

To make the sauce, add the tea bags, pepper, cinnamon stick, soy sauce, five-spice powder, ginger, and chiles (if using).

Bring to a boil. Turn the heat to low, cover the pan, and simmer for 40 minutes.

Remove from the heat. Let the eggs steep in the sauce for 12 hours or overnight.

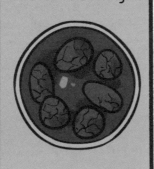

To serve, peel the eggs and remove any membrane.

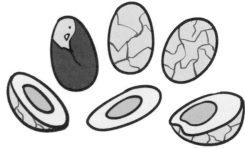

Serve sliced, quartered, or whole, at room temperature or chilled.

Leftover eggs can be stored in the sauce, in a tightly sealed container in the refrigerator for up to 3 days.

# YING-YANG RICE BALLS

The concept of yin and yang is from ancient Chinese culture. It describes two opposite yet interdependent parts that represent the universe. The complementary pairing depicts a balance of all the forces of existence: sun and moon, female and male, summer and winter, water and fire, light and dark, white and black. The concept of yin and yang guides every aspect of daily life in China, from personal relationships to cuisine.

Yin-yang rice balls was one of my favorite dishes growing up, yet it is connected to one of my least favorite times: China's Cultural Revolution.

When I was in elementary school, once a week we were required to attend the "reeducation class for the youth." On that day, my classmates and I would report to school at dawn and go to a farm outside of the city to weed vegetable fields.

On days when the weather was especially frigid and harsh, Nai Nai would make yin-yang rice balls for me.

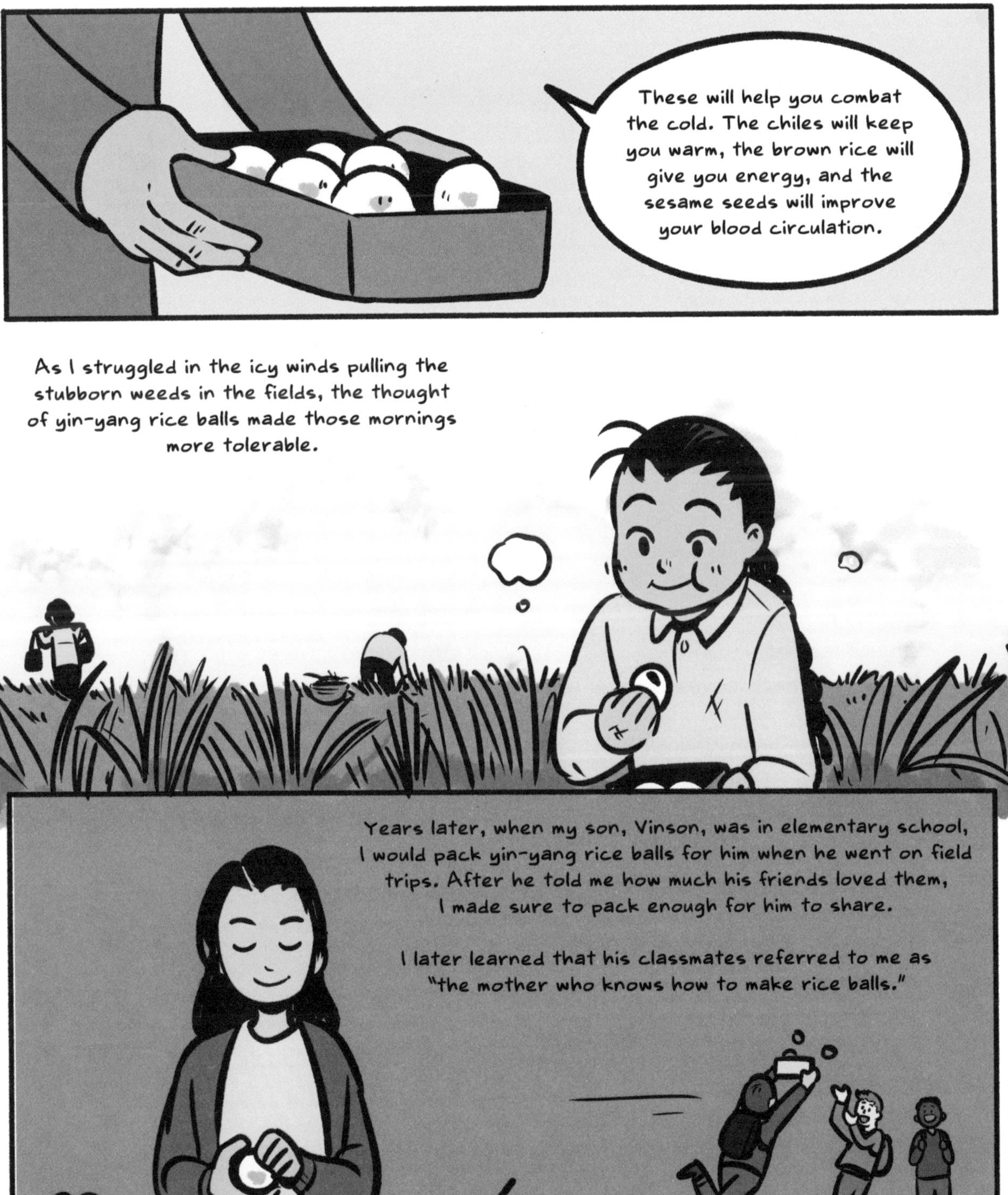
These will help you combat the cold. The chiles will keep you warm, the brown rice will give you energy, and the sesame seeds will improve your blood circulation.
As I struggled in the icy winds pulling the stubborn weeds in the fields, the thought of yin-yang rice balls made those mornings more tolerable.
Years later, when my son, Vinson, was in elementary school, I would pack yin-yang rice balls for him when he went on field trips. After he told me how much his friends loved them, I made sure to pack enough for him to share.
I later learned that his classmates referred to me as "the mother who knows how to make rice balls."

# YIN-YANG RICE BALLS
## （阴阳饭团）

This was one of my favorite childhood dishes that Nai Nai made. I serve them as appetizers at dinner parties and pack them as snacks when I go on hikes with friends and family. To complement the spicy rice balls, I created a sweet version. Serve both as a striking appetizer for a dinner party or with afternoon tea. You can find sweet brown and white rice in Asian grocery stores and health food stores.

**Makes 6 servings**

**Brown Rice Mixture**

3 black tea bags

1½ cups spinach leaves or other leafy greens

1 Tbsp extra-virgin olive oil

½ cup store-bought baked tofu, minced

¼ cup minced carrots

1 tsp minced fresh red chile

2 green onions, green parts only, minced

2 cups cooked sweet brown rice

2 tsp sesame oil

1 tsp freshly ground black pepper

**White Rice Mixture**

2 cups cooked sweet white rice, warm

¼ cup dried cherries, minced

¼ cup dried dates, minced

3 Tbsp honey or maple syrup

1½ cups black sesame seeds, toasted

1½ cups white sesame seeds, toasted

Banana leaves, for serving

# HOW TO MAKE YIN-YANG RICE BALLS

To make the brown rice mixture, in a small pot, bring 4 cups of water to a boil over high heat.

Add the tea bags and spinach leaves.

Blanch until the spinach leaves are soft, about 15 seconds; be careful not to overcook.

Remove the tea bags and discard.

Drain and rinse the spinach under cold running water.

Squeeze the spinach to remove the excess water. Mince.

In a wok or nonstick skillet, heat the olive oil over medium-high heat.

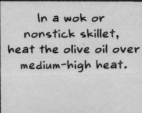

Add the tofu, carrots, and chile and sauté until the tofu browns, about 2 minutes.

Add the prepared spinach and green onions and stir-fry for 1 minute.

Stir in the brown rice, sesame oil, and black pepper. Mix thoroughly and let the rice heat through.

Transfer the mixture to a bowl and set aside to cool slightly.

## PART 2

To make the white rice mixture, in a large mixing bowl, combine the white rice, cherries, dates, and honey.

To assemble, pour the black and white sesame seeds into two separate shallow bowls. Line a serving plate with banana leaves. If you don't have banana leaves, lightly oil the serving plate.

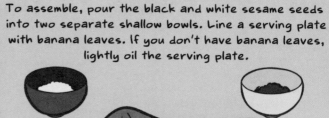

With wet hands, tightly pack about ¼ cup of the brown rice mixture into a ball.

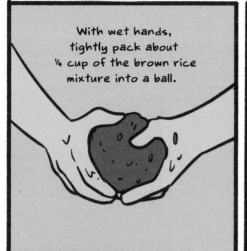

Roll it in the black sesame seeds until coated and place it on the serving plate.

Repeat with the remaining brown rice mixture.

In the same manner, form the white rice mixture into balls and roll in the white sesame seeds.

Artfully arrange the spicy and sweet rice balls on the plate. Serve at room temperature.

To store, seal leftovers in an airtight container and refrigerate for up to 3 days.

# CHOPSTICKS HACK: WRAPS TO THE RESCUE!

Growing up in Wuhan, China, I spent many hours of my childhood following Nai Nai around our kitchen. I enjoyed watching her slice meat, boil dumplings, and cut tofu. Her skillful knife cutting turned bamboo shoots into trees, green onions into brushes, white onions into roses, and carrots and icicle radishes into blossoms. Best of all, I got to taste what Nai Nai cooked before my brothers did.

I was four years old when Nai Nai gave me a pair of small, red, training chopsticks.

They were tied together at the top with a rubber band to help me learn to use them.

That same day, Nai Nai served rice noodles for lunch.

Ugh!

PLOP

I am done with sticks!

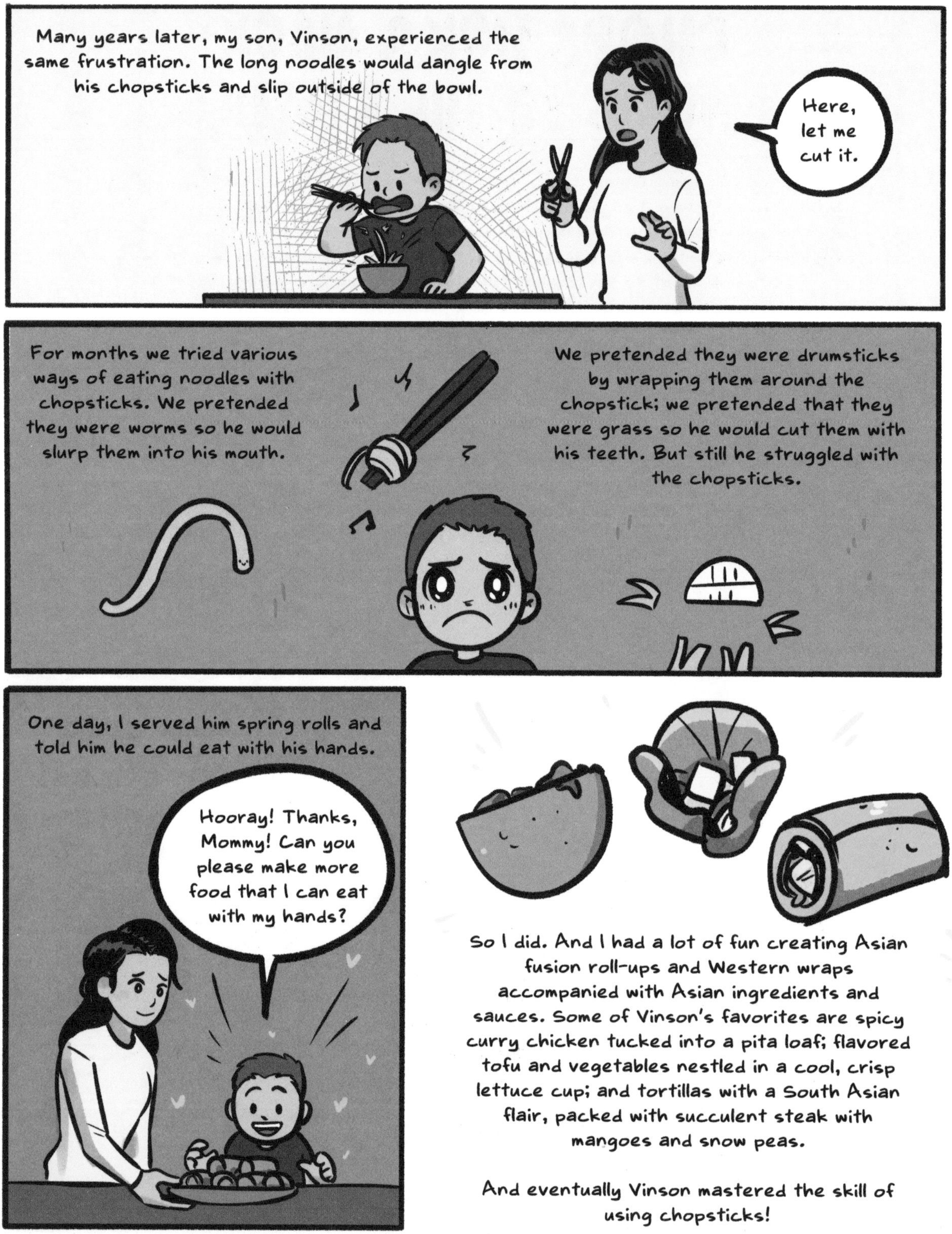
Many years later, my son, Vinson, experienced the same frustration. The long noodles would dangle from his chopsticks and slip outside of the bowl.
Here, let me cut it.
For months we tried various ways of eating noodles with chopsticks. We pretended they were worms so he would slurp them into his mouth.
We pretended they were drumsticks by wrapping them around the chopstick; we pretended that they were grass so he would cut them with his teeth. But still he struggled with the chopsticks.
One day, I served him spring rolls and told him he could eat with his hands.
Hooray! Thanks, Mommy! Can you please make more food that I can eat with my hands?
So I did. And I had a lot of fun creating Asian fusion roll-ups and Western wraps accompanied with Asian ingredients and sauces. Some of Vinson's favorites are spicy curry chicken tucked into a pita loaf; flavored tofu and vegetables nestled in a cool, crisp lettuce cup; and tortillas with a South Asian flair, packed with succulent steak with mangoes and snow peas.
And eventually Vinson mastered the skill of using chopsticks!

# MANGO—LOBSTER SPRING ROLLS
## (芒果龙虾春卷)

This is one of Vinson's favorite dishes. When fresh lobster is not available, I simply substitute crabmeat or shrimp for a delicious twist. These spring rolls are perfect for any party appetizer spread. Double the fun by inviting your friends over for a spring roll assembly party!

**Makes 12 rolls**

**Green Tea Orange Sauce**

¼ cup extra-virgin olive oil

1 Tbsp grated orange zest

2 tsp loose green tea, such as gunpowder

⅓ cup soy sauce

3 Tbsp rice vinegar

4 green onions, white parts only, minced

**Filling**

2 Tbsp fish sauce

1 Tbsp rice wine or dry sherry

3½ tsp peeled and minced fresh ginger

1 Tbsp chopped fresh cilantro

8 oz cooked lobster meat, broken into chunks

2 Tbsp extra-virgin olive oil

1 Tbsp loose green tea, such as gunpowder

2 small mangoes, peeled, pitted, and diced

Twelve 8 in round dried rice paper wrappers

# HOW TO MAKE MANGO-LOBSTER SPRING ROLLS

## SAUCE

To make the sauce, in a small saucepan over medium heat, heat the oil.
Add the orange zest and green tea, and sauté until fragrant.

Remove from the heat. Stir in the soy sauce, vinegar, and green onions. Let it cool.

Refrigerate in a tightly sealed glass container for 30 minutes or overnight to allow the flavors to meld.
It can last in the refrigerator for up to 5 days.

## FILLING

To make the filling, in a medium bowl, combine the fish sauce, rice wine, 1½ tsp of the ginger, and the cilantro.

Add the lobster meat and toss to combine. Cover and marinate in the refrigerator for 30 minutes.

In a wok or nonstick skillet over medium-high heat, heat the oil and swirl to coat.

Add the green tea and sauté until fragrant, about 30 seconds.

Add the remaining 2 tsp of ginger and sauté for another 30 seconds.

Add the lobster mixture and toss until it is heated through, about 1 minute.

Remove from the
heat and set aside.
Once the mixture is cool,
stir in the mangoes.

To make the spring rolls,
fill a medium bowl with warm water.
Dip a rice paper wrapper into
the water for 15 seconds or
until softened.

Carefully transfer it
to a dry work surface.

Arrange 2 to 3 Tbsp of the
filling in an even horizontal
mound just below the
center of the wrapper.

Roll up the rice paper to form a tight cylinder,
folding in the sides about halfway.
Assemble the remaining spring rolls
in the same manner.

Cover the finished rolls
with a damp cloth
to prevent them
from drying out.

Serve the rolls at room temperature
with the green tea orange sauce.

To store, wrap each roll in plastic wrap
and refrigerate in an airtight container for up to 2 days.

# CRISPY SHRIMP SPRING ROLLS
## (脆皮虾春卷)

When I was growing up in China during the Cultural Revolution, I never had a birthday cake because it was considered Western and bourgeois. Instead, my mother made these spring rolls for my birthday celebration. The sauce can be made ahead. For a smoother texture, purée it in a blender.

**Makes 20 rolls**

**Thai Sauce**
2 Tbsp almond butter or peanut butter
½ cup plain soy milk
¼ cup low-fat unsweetened coconut milk
2 Tbsp fresh lime juice
1 Tbsp fish sauce
1 Tbsp honey
4 garlic cloves, minced
1 medium fresh red chile, such as Fresno, seeded and minced
1 green onion, minced
1 Tbsp chopped fresh cilantro

**Shrimp**

1 Tbsp rice wine or medium-dry sherry
1 Tbsp fish sauce
1½ tsp fresh lemon juice
1 Tbsp chopped fresh cilantro
1 small fresh red chile, such as Fresno, seeded and minced
3 garlic cloves, minced
2 tsp peeled and minced fresh ginger
1 lb medium shrimp, peeled and deveined

**Peach Mixture**

1 large peach or apple, peeled and diced
4 green onions, green parts only, sliced into thin slivers
1 small red bell pepper, seeded and diced
1 small yellow bell pepper, seeded and diced
1 Tbsp rice vinegar
1½ tsp toasted sesame oil

Twenty 8 in dried rice paper wrappers
20 fresh basil leaves
1 head Bibb lettuce, leaves washed and separated

# HOW TO MAKE CRISPY SHRIMP SPRING ROLLS

**THAI SAUCE**

To make the thai sauce, place the almond butter in a medium bowl.

Slowly whisk in the soy milk, coconut milk, lime juice, fish sauce, and honey until smooth.

Stir in the garlic, chile, green onion, and cilantro.

Cover and refrigerate for 30 minutes or overnight to allow the flavors to blend.

**SHRIMP**

To prepare the shrimp, combine the rice wine, fish sauce, lemon juice, cilantro, chile, garlic, and ginger in a medium bowl.

Add the shrimp and toss to coat.

Cover and marinate in the refrigerator for 30 minutes or up to overnight.

**PEACH**

To make the peach mixture, in a medium bowl, combine the peach, green onions, red and yellow bell peppers, vinegar, and sesame oil.

Toss to coat.

Fill a medium bowl with warm water. Dip a rice paper wrapper into the water for 15 seconds or until softened.

Carefully transfer it to a dry work surface.

Center a basil leaf in the bottom third of the wrapper.
Top with three shrimps and 2 Tbsp of the peach mixture.

Fold the wrapper over the filling and roll it into a tight cylinder, folding in the sides about halfway.

Assemble the remaining rolls the same way.

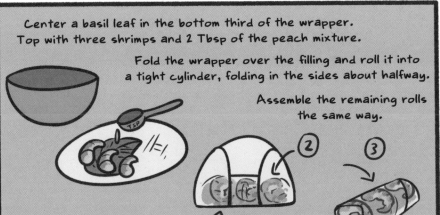

Cover the finished rolls with a damp cloth to prevent them from drying out.

Preheat the broiler to 450°F.

Lightly coat a large nonstick baking sheet with extra-virgin olive oil cooking spray.

Arrange the spring rolls on the baking sheet in a single layer, leaving a little space between them. Lightly coat the rolls with cooking spray.

Broil the rolls until lightly browned and crisp, about 10 minutes. Using tongs or a spatula, turn the rolls over and continue to broil for another 8 to 10 minutes.

Serve each roll warm, wrapped in lettuce leaves with Thai sauce for dipping.

To store, refrigerate the remaining rolls in an airtight container for up to 3 days.

Chapter 2

# Main Cours
# (主菜)

es

# BEGGAR'S CHICKEN

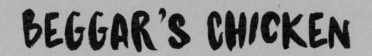

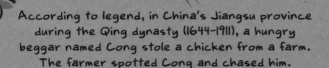

According to legend, in China's Jiangsu province during the Qing dynasty (1644–1911), a hungry beggar named Cong stole a chicken from a farm. The farmer spotted Cong and chased him.

Cong made it to a river and, in desperation, quickly buried the chicken in the wet, muddy bank.

He hid among the reeds until sunset. When the moon rose, Cong returned to the bank, relieved that the farmer had gone.

Shivering from cold and hunger, he lit a torch and dug out his chicken, now coated with mud.

Too weak to wash off the mud, he placed it over an open flame. Soon the heat from the fire hardened the mud into clay.

Cong used a small rock to break it off. To his delight, all the feathers fell right off the chicken!

He took a bite. The meat was juicy and came right off the bone. It was the best meat he'd ever had.

With a full tummy, an idea formed in his mind. He wrapped the remaining half chicken and sold it to a villager.

With the money, Cong bought a chicken, cooked it the same way, and sold it at the market. With that money, he bought more chickens and sold those too.

Eventually he made enough money to open a restaurant selling "beggar's chicken."

News of this dish spread so far and wide that it reached Emperor Kangxi. The emperor traveled to Cong's restaurant.

He loved the chicken so much that he added it to the imperial court's menu. From there, beggar's chicken gained notoriety across all of China.

# BEGGAR'S CHICKEN
## （乞丐鸡）

This recipe is well worth the time it requires. The lotus leaves and clay lend the chicken a fresh fragrance and an unearthly tenderness. Cooks often stuff the chicken with their favorite filling and encase it in clay before baking. When proper clay is not available, I substitute it with flour dough (see page 49). If you're using chicken breast only, stuff each breast with one quarter of the rice mixture and wrap each breast with lotus leaves, baking for 1½ hours. Both results are equally delicious. Just like hungry Cong, you'll be "begging" for more!

### Makes 4 servings

¼ cup dark soy sauce, plus more for serving
3 Tbsp rice wine or dry sherry
1½ tsp five-spice powder
One 2½ lb whole chicken or 4½ lb chicken breasts
½ cup glutinous rice
2 dried lotus leaves, about 18 in long and 10 in wide
2 dried shiitake mushrooms
⅓ cup extra-virgin olive oil
1½ Tbsp peeled and minced fresh ginger
3 garlic cloves, chopped
3 Tbsp water chestnuts, chopped
2 green onions, white parts only, sliced
11 lb (approximately) food-safe sculptor's or potter's earth clay

# HOW TO MAKE BEGGAR'S CHICKEN

**PART 1**

To make the marinade, in a small bowl, combine the soy sauce, rice wine, and five-spice powder.

Pat the chicken dry with a paper towel.

Place the chicken in a large bowl and rub the skin and cavity with the soy mixture.

Cover and refrigerate overnight.

**PART 2**

In a medium lidded bowl, cover the glutinous rice with water and let it rest overnight.

The next day, drain the chicken, reserving 2 Tbsp of the marinade, and let it rest for about 30 minutes.

Drain the rice.

In a large bowl filled with warm water, soak the lotus leaves until soft, about 30 minutes.

Meanwhile, in a small bowl, cover the shiitakes with water and soak until the caps are softened, about 15 minutes.

Drain and squeeze to extract excess moisture.

Discard this liquid.

Cut off the tough stems and discard.

Cut the caps into thin slivers and set aside.

In a wok over medium-high heat, heat the oil.

Cook the ginger and garlic until fragrant, about 1 minute.

Stir in the shiitake caps, water chestnuts, green onions, glutinous rice, and the reserved marinade. Toss until heated through.

Remove from the heat and let the mixture sit until it's cool enough to handle.

**PART 3**

Preheat the oven to 350°F. Line a rimmed baking sheet with foil.

Stuff the rice mixture into the chicken's cavity.

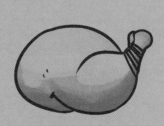

Truss the chicken with kitchen twine, folding the wing tips under the chicken.

# PART 4

To prepare the chicken, remove the lotus leaves from the water and lay them on a flat surface. Make sure that they overlap in a triangle formation.

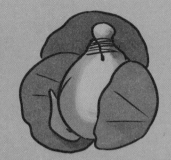

Place the chicken in the center and wrap it tightly in the leaves.

Use kitchen twine to secure the leaves around the chicken.

Cover the chicken with a ¼ in thick layer of clay, pressing as you work, until the chicken is completely covered with a smooth layer of clay.

Place the chicken on the prepared baking sheet.

Bake for 3 hours at 350°F.

Remove the chicken from the oven. Let it cool for about 30 minutes.

If the clay cracks, the chicken is done. Alternatively, insert a thermometer through the clay through the thickest part of the chicken; it should read 165°F.

To serve, break open the clay shell with a hammer and discard the lotus leaves.

Carve the chicken and serve it warm with soy sauce.

## FLOUR DOUGH VARIATION

Ingredients
- 4 cups all-purpose flour (plus more for dusting)
- 3¼ cups kosher salt
- 2 pinches five-spice powder

**PART 4.5**

Prepare the chicken and soak the lotus leaves as described in the clay variation.

In a large bowl, combine the flour, salt, and five-spice powder; mix well.

Add 1½ cups of water, and use your hands to mix and knead it into a firm dough. Add more water if needed, 1 Tbsp at a time, until the mixture forms into a soft dough.

Lay out the lotus leaves on a flat surface. Make sure that they overlap in a triangle formation.

Place the chicken in the center and wrap it tightly in the leaves. Use kitchen twine to secure the leaves around the chicken.

Place the dough onto a lightly floured work surface and knead until smooth, about 5 minutes. Roll the dough into a 15 in round, approximately 1 in thick.

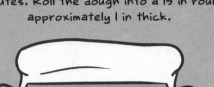

Place the chicken in the center of the dough and wrap it to cover, sealing the edges to ensure that there are no tears.

Place the chicken on the prepared baking sheet. Bake and serve as in the clay variation.

# DAN DAN NOODLES

In recent years, Sichuan cuisine has spread all over the world. If you have been to a Sichuan restaurant, chances are you have come across dan dan noodles (担担面). Many seasoned foodies use this dish to judge a restaurant's caliber.

In Chinese, dan dan means "bamboo carrying pole." These poles were used by walking street vendors, who would attach two baskets to a pole-one holding the ingredients and utensils, while the other carried a small, portable stove. This portable setup allowed the vendor to serve noodles whenever they encountered a customer.

According to legend, in 1841 BC, there was a poor peddler named Chen BaoBao who lived in Chengdu, the capital of Sichuan. BaoBao lost his parents at a young age and lived with his grandmother. He grew into a strong and kind young man, and helped his grandmother sell noodles on a busy street outside their home.

As more vendors set up stalls on the street, BaoBao and his grandmother were selling fewer and fewer bowls of noodles. It hurt BaoBao a great deal to see his grandma worried.

One day, he had an idea.

What are you doing?

There are too many vendors in the center of the city. I am going to sell our noodles in the quiet streets.

But that is a heavy load!

Don't worry, Grandma, I am strong.

BaoBao walked to a quiet neighborhood on the outskirts of the city. There were no other vendors in sight.

Hot and spicy nooooodles! Hot and tasty nooooodles!

The aromatic scent of the spices drifted into open windows. People ran out, bowls and pots in hand. They gathered around BaoBao's stand, eager to try it.

Oh, these are the best noodles I have ever had!

It's so nice I can taste something so good right outside my home. I can't walk far with my bound feet.

The vegetable topping complements the hot and spicy noodles so nicely.

That day BaoBao sold out of his noodles. When he returned the next day, the moment he shouted, "Hot and spicy nooooodles!" people ran out of their homes. Soon BaoBao's noodles gained notoriety and became the talk of the town.

Eventually BaoBao made enough money to open a restaurant selling noodles with his grandma, and the name "dan dan noodles" spread all over Sichuan and the world.

# DAN DAN NOODLES
## (担担面)

---

This ubiquitous dish has many variations, but a common trait is its thick, spicy sauce that gives a distinctive nutty, hot, and numbing taste. It's usually topped with fried minced meat, preserved vegetables, and fried peanuts. If you'd like to enjoy the taste of authentic Sichuan street food in the comfort of your home, give this recipe a try!

**Makes 4 servings**

1 Tbsp extra-virgin olive oil
8 oz ground pork
2 tsp hoisin sauce
2 tsp rice wine or dry sherry
1 tsp plus 3 Tbsp soy sauce, plus more as needed
¾ tsp five-spice powder
½ cup black sesame paste or tahini
¼ cup chili oil, plus more as needed
4½ tsp peeled and minced fresh ginger
2 garlic cloves, minced
2 tsp granulated sugar
½ tsp ground Sichuan peppercorns
8 oz thin fresh or dry Chinese wheat noodles
1 tsp sesame oil
12 oz bok choy, cleaned, ends trimmed
Chopped green onions, for garnishing
Chopped peanuts, for garnishing (optional)

---

# HOW TO MAKE DAN DAN NOODLES

## PART 1

To cook the ground pork, in a wok over medium heat, heat the olive oil.

Add the pork. Cook and stir until it's brown.

Add the hoisin sauce, rice wine, 1 tsp of the soy sauce, and ½ tsp of the five-spice powder. Cook and stir until the liquid has evaporated.

Remove from the heat and set aside.

## PART 2

To make the sauce, in a medium bowl, combine the sesame paste, chili oil, remaining 3 Tbsp of soy sauce, ginger, garlic, sugar, peppercorns, and the remaining ¼ tsp of five-spice powder. Set aside.

## PART 3

In a large pot, cook the noodles according to the package directions. Reserve at least ½ cup of the cooking liquid and drain the rest.

Rinse the noodles under cold water and drain again.

In a serving bowl, toss the noodles with the sesame oil.

In a large pot, bring water to a boil and blanch the bok choy for 2 minutes. Drain.

Add ¼ cup of the reserved noodle water to the sauce. Taste and adjust the seasoning and texture with more soy sauce, chili oil, and hot noodle water if needed.

To serve, in four bowls, divide the noodles, sauce, and bok choy.

Top each with one quarter of the pork mixture.

Sprinkle with the green onions and peanuts (if using). Toss each bowl well and serve.

To store, seal leftovers in an airtight container and refrigerate for up to 3 days.

# DONGPO PORK

During the Song dynasty (960–1279), the famous poet and calligrapher Su Dongpo wrote a poem expressing criticisms of Chancellor Wang Anshi's reformist policies.

Although Anshi and Dongpo reconciled in private, members of Anshi's policy group slandered Dongpo in front of Emperor Shenzong, accusing him of criticizing the emperor. Shenzong exiled Dongpo to a remote village in the Hubei province.

Dongpo spent his days writing and reciting poems in his unheated room.

*The spring river wants to flood the house.*

*The force of the rain is unrelenting.*

*My small house is like a fishing boat in the midst of fog and water.*

*In an empty kitchen, I boil cold vegetables on a broken stove burning damp reeds . . .*

Dongpo didn't miss the politics of the Song court, but he longed for a bowl of hot meat stew on a cold day. Without pay, his savings dwindled down to a few coins.

On the day his good friend Qin was coming for a visit, Dongpo took his last few coins and walked through heavy rain and wind to buy a piece of pork belly and a bottle of rice wine.

When he arrived home, he immediately got to cooking the meal for his friend. He lit his small stove, filled a clay pot with water, and laid green onions and ginger on the bottom. He carefully laid the meat on top and covered it with soy sauce, rice wine, and fermented bean paste. The smell reminded Dongpo of the elaborate meals he once ate at court.

After the two friends greeted each other warmly, they sat down to play a game of Go. In between moves, Dongpo recited his new poem, "Water Melody," to his friend with tears down his face.

When will the moon be clear and bright?

With a cup of wine in my hand,
I ask the clear sky.

In the heavens on this night,
I wonder what season it would be?

I want to ride the wind to fly home . . .

May we all be blessed with longevity,

Though thousands of miles apart,
we are still able to share the beauty of the moon together.

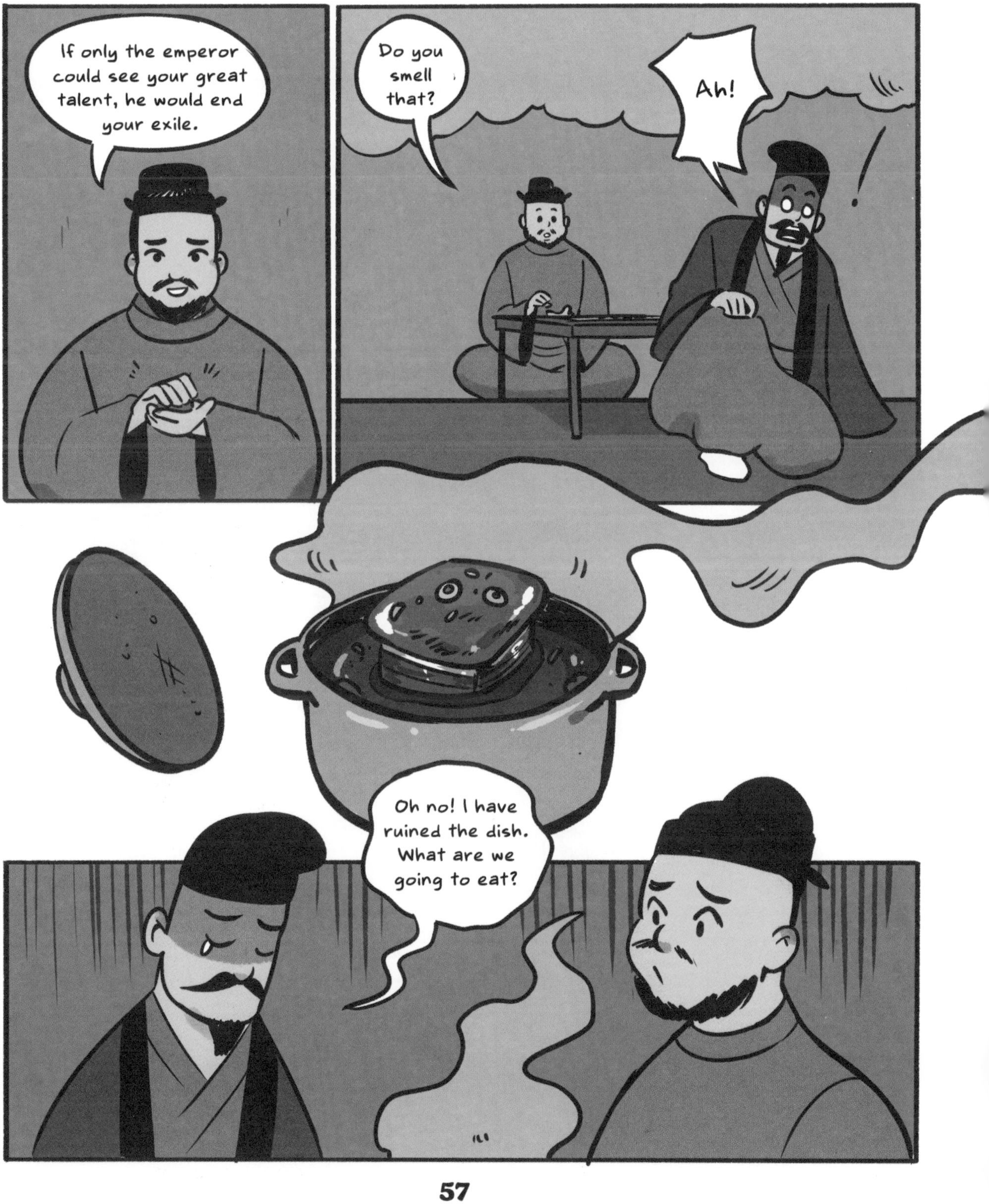
If only the emperor could see your great talent, he would end your exile.
Do you smell that?
Ah!
Oh no! I have ruined the dish. What are we going to eat?

It smells delicious, let's try it!

This is the best meat dish I've ever had! Can you please share the recipe?

I will need some time to write it up.

The two friends enjoyed a hearty meal. When Qin returned to court, he went to the emperor, praising Dongpo's talent as well as his delicious pork.

Eventually the emperor ended Dongpo's exile. And before long, "Dongpo pork" became famous in China and gained popularity around the world.

# DONGPO PORK
## （东坡肉）

Dongpo pork, also called dong po rou or braised pork belly, is an ideal dish to share with family or friends on a cold night. This simple, hearty dish requires little effort. The key to its success lies in the sauce. After marinating the pork in its rich and tasty sauce, it becomes flavorful inside and out. Do it right and you might "hog" this dish for yourself!

**Makes 6 servings**

2 lb pork belly
1½ Tbsp extra-virgin olive oil
5 green onions, cut into ½ in pieces
8 slices fresh ginger
¼ cup rock sugar
2 cups rice wine or dry sherry
⅔ cup soy sauce
2½ Tbsp fermented red chili bean curd

# HOW TO MAKE DONGPO PORK

Bring a large pot of water to a boil.

Add the pork belly. Bring the water back to a boil and let the pork belly cook for 3 minutes.

Drain and dry it with paper towels.

In a wok or large cast-iron pan over medium-high heat, heat the oil.

Brown the pork belly on all sides.

In a medium pot, lay the green onions on the bottom.

Place the ginger slices evenly over the green onions and then lay the pork belly, skin-side down, on top.

To make the sauce, in a small pot over low heat, mix ½ cup of water and the rock sugar.

Cook and stir until the sugar is dissolved.

Turn off the heat and stir in the rice wine, soy sauce, and bean curd.

Pour the sauce over the pork belly and bring it to a boil.

Once boiling, cover the pot and turn down the heat to low. Let it simmer for 1 hour. Check occasionally.

If the sauce starts to dry up, add more water or soy sauce.

After an hour, turn the pork belly skin-side up in the pot, cover, and let simmer for another hour.

To serve, transfer the pork pieces to a plate, drizzling the remaining sauce over the meat.

To store, seal leftovers in an airtight container and refrigerate for up to 5 days.

# IGNORED BY DOGGY BUNS

Many years ago, an old couple named Wu were returning home from the market. As they were passing through the streets of their little town outside Tianjin, they saw two dogs chasing a young boy.

Mr. Wu waved the dogs away with his cane.

SHOO, GO AWAY!

Though the threat was gone, the boy still kept his distance from the couple.

Kind Mrs. Wu offered the young boy a piece of sweet potato.

The boy was a street orphan. He was so shy and traumatized he couldn't even muster the will to thank the couple for the sweet potato.

The Wus continued their walk but noticed that the boy was following them. Touched by his plight, they adopted him.

Because of his nature, the couple decided to name the boy Gou, or "Doggy."

Being an orphan in his early years, Gou never got enough to eat. This hunger led to a true appreciation for food.

He liked to help Mrs. Wu in the kitchen and gradually took over the task of cooking for the family.

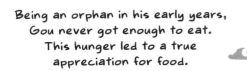

Although he rarely spoke, he was very deferential to the Wus. When he was fourteen, Mr. Wu spoke to Gou.

We are getting old, you will have to learn a skill to support yourself.

What would you like to be?

A cook!

So the following week, Gou was sent to be an apprentice at a steamed bun shop in Tianjin.

chop chop

Gou worked hard, spending his days in the kitchen, washing and chopping meat and vegetables.

Soon he gained the trust of the restaurant owner, who taught him the secret of making delicious meat fillings and puffy dough for his tantalizing steam buns.

A year later, when Gou returned to his adoptive parents, he found they were too weak to work in the fields. Gou decided to set up a stall selling steamed pork buns-baozi to support them.

I want to start my own business, selling baozi.

The Wus could not decide which was more surprising, that Gou had just spoken such a long sentence, or that he had such ambitious plans. How could Gou run a business if he never talked to his customers?

Despite their doubts, the Wus went around the village borrowing money for Gou to open his stall. Gou set up a sign next to a wooden box in front of his stove.

On the sign, he marked the price of his baozi and instructed the customers to leave their payment in the box.

The very first day, customers fell in love with Gou's puffy, tasty buns and juicy filling. From then on, a long line formed every morning, as soon as Gou set up his stall.

Gou was always busy. No matter who tried to talk to him, he studiously ignored them, focusing on rolling dough, mixing the meat filling, or making the buns.

Over time, customers grew used to dealing with the silent Gou.

PAY HERE →

They named his buns goubuli baozi, or ignored by doggy buns.

# IGNORED BY DOGGY BUNS
## (狗不理包子)

Baozi is a classic bun stuffed with minced pork and vegetables that's either pan-fried or steamed. It's a popular staple served by street vendors throughout China. Baozi are served as an alternative to rice or noodles for meals or as a snack.

**Makes 12 buns**

8 oz lean ground pork, beef, or turkey
3 large napa cabbage leaves, stemmed and minced
3 green onions, minced
3 Tbsp soy sauce
2 Tbsp rice wine or dry sherry
1 Tbsp peeled and minced fresh ginger
½ Tbsp toasted sesame oil
1½ cups all-purpose flour or cake flour, or 12 canned biscuits
3 Tbsp extra-virgin olive oil
1½ tsp dried yeast
1 tsp granulated sugar

# HOW TO MAKE IGNORED BY DOGGY BUNS

**FILLING**

To make the filling, in a large bowl combine the pork, cabbage, green onions, soy sauce, rice wine, ginger, and sesame oil.

Cover and refrigerate for 30 minutes.

**DOUGH**

To make the dough, in a large bowl combine the flour, 1 Tbsp of the olive oil, yeast, and sugar.

Pour in ¾ cup of lukewarm water a little at a time while mixing the dough with your hands. Knead the dough until smooth.

Cover with a damp cloth, and leave it in a warm place until it doubles in size, about 1 hour.

Place the raised dough on a lightly floured surface. Knead it again to remove any bubbles trapped inside. Divide the dough into 12 equal portions.

To assemble, roll a piece of dough or one biscuit into a 4 in round.

Place about 2 Tbsp of filling in the center of the dough.

Gather up and close the dough edges over the filling, and twist the tops to seal.

Place the bun, twisted-side up, on a floured plate. Repeat with the remaining dough portions and filling.

Preheat the oven to 300°F.

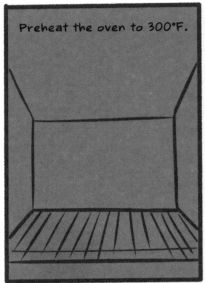

In a large nonstick skillet over medium-low heat, add ¼ cup of water and 1 Tbsp of the olive oil.

Place half of the buns, twisted-side up and not touching, in the skillet.

Cover and cook until the buns puff up and are light brown on the bottom, 8 to 10 minutes.

Transfer the buns to a baking sheet and place them in the oven to keep warm.

Repeat with the remaining buns, another ¼ cup of water, and the remaining 1 Tbsp of olive oil. Serve hot.

To store, seal leftover buns in an airtight container and refrigerate for up to 3 days.

# LION'S HEAD MEATBALLS

If you've ever attended a Chinese family gathering or a banquet, chances are you've seen lion's head meatballs. You may wonder how they got their name. The dish's alternate name, sunflower minced meat, doesn't tell the story either.

The legend goes that Emperor Yang from the Sui dynasty (581–618) ordered the construction of the Grand Canal to link various rivers that stretch from Beijing to Hangzhou.

The emperor traveled to different regions along the canal. When he got to Yangzhou City, in today's Jiangsu province, he was captivated by a splendid valley of vibrant gold sunflowers.

After returning to his capital city of Xian, he was still reminiscing about the beauty of the flowers.

Remember those beautiful sunflowers we saw in Yangzhou? Could you create a flavorful dish that resembles their beauty?

Yes, your majesty. I will do my best.

In the following days, the chef experimented with many ingredients until he finally came up with something that could work.

He minced some pork and mixed it with ginger, green onions, water chestnuts, and spices.

He then molded it into large meatballs, which formed an interesting pattern from the mixture of lean and fatty meat.

He dropped the balls into hot oil. When he scooped out the deep-fried meatballs, he was thrilled that they had turned golden outside with a texture resembling sunflowers.

To make it more flavorful, he cooked them in a soy-ginger-wine broth in a clay pot.

Emperor Yang was amazed by the appearance of the meatballs that resembled sunflowers and fell in love with their juicy tenderness.

Through the years, "sunflower minced meat" became known as "lion's head meatballs." Some people believe it's due to the meatballs' large size, while others think it's because eating the savory meatballs gives people the strength of a lion.

The most popular theory is that the crinkled-up napa cabbage lined in the clay pot of the broth reminds people of a lion's mane.

Only one thing is for certain: Regardless of the name, this dish is sure to give you strength and satisfy your taste buds!

# LION'S HEAD MEATBALLS

## (狮子头)

Even the pickiest eaters will roar for more of these meatballs! To save time, cook them a day or two in advance. Store them covered in the refrigerator and reheat them in the sauce just before serving. Leftover meatballs will absorb the ginger-coconut sauce and be even more flavorful the next day.

### Makes 8 large meatballs

½ cup unsweetened light coconut milk

½ cup soy milk

2 Tbsp Thai fish sauce

3 Tbsp peeled and minced fresh ginger

1 Tbsp plus ½ cup chopped green onions, white parts only

4 tsp seeded and minced hot red chile

1 lb lean ground pork or beef

2 oz leeks, white and light green parts, minced

2 Tbsp cornstarch

1 Tbsp all-purpose flour

2 Tbsp sesame oil

½ tsp salt

¼ tsp ground white pepper

2 Tbsp extra-virgin olive oil

1 medium head iceberg or Boston lettuce

¼ cup fresh basil or Thai basil leaves, chopped, and 1 Tbsp grated lemon zest, for garnishing

# HOW TO MAKE LION'S HEAD MEATBALLS

To make the sauce, in a small bowl, combine the coconut milk, soy milk, fish sauce, 2 Tbsp of the ginger, 1 Tbsp of the green onions, and 2 tsp of the chile. Set aside.

FISH Sauce

Soy MILK

COCONUT MILK

Oil a plate and set aside.

To make the meatballs, in a large mixing bowl, combine the pork, the remaining ½ cup of green onions, leeks, the remaining 1 Tbsp of ginger, cornstarch, flour, sesame oil, the remaining 2 tsp of chile, salt, and white pepper.

Mix by hand until the ingredients are thoroughly combined and the mixture becomes sticky.

Divide into 8 equal portions.

Roll each portion into a ball and set it on the oiled plate.

In a wok or nonstick skillet over medium-high heat, warm the oil and swirl to coat.

Add the meatballs and cook over medium heat, turning occasionally, until browned on all sides.

Transfer to paper towels to drain.

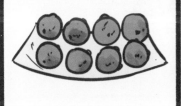

In a large saucepan over medium-high heat bring the sauce to a boil.

Add the meatballs, cover, and reduce the heat to low.

Simmer until cooked through, about 8 minutes.

Arrange the lettuce leaves on a serving platter.

Nestle the meatballs in the middle. Garnish with the basil and lemon zest and serve warm.

To store, seal leftovers in an airtight container and refrigerate for up to 3 days.

# OLD POCKMARKED LADY'S MAPO TOFU

During the Qing dynasty (1644-1911), in north Chengdu, Mr. and Mrs. Chen owned a small restaurant called Xingsheng. It was located near the busy Wanfu Bridge, a popular resting place for oil porters, rickshaw drivers, and laborers.

When Mrs. Chen was a child, she was infected with smallpox, which left her face scarred with many pockmarks.

For a long time, Mrs. Chen felt insecure about her face. So she stayed in the back kitchen cooking to avoid interacting with the customers while Mr. Chen tended to the front.

Mr. Chen died unexpectedly, leaving Mrs. Chen to look after Xingsheng alone.

On a rainy, cold night, Mrs. Chen paced around the empty restaurant.

My face will scare off the customers! What should I do?

Suddenly a group of oil porters came through the front door.

Could you please use these ingredients to cook something for us?

We didn't make much money today, but we have enough to pay you for your labor.

Mrs. Chen nodded and took the ingredients into her kitchen. Soon she emerged with a big tray.

On it were a big bamboo basket of cooked rice and a big bowl of steaming hot tofu swimming in a fragrant red meat sauce garnished with minced green onions.

Soon the word of a delicious tofu dish cooked by an old lady with a pockmarked face spread throughout the region. People from near and far came to eat mapo tofu at Xingsheng. Before long, the tongue-tingling, flavorful tofu spread all over the world—and Mrs. Chen changed her restaurant's name to Chen Mapo.

# OLD POCKMARKED LADY'S MAPO TOFU (麻婆豆腐)

In this savory dish, the tofu is cooked in an aromatic, spicy sauce. Serve it with black or brown rice for a hearty and healthy meal. Feel free to adjust the spiciness to your preference. For vegetarians, replace the meat with shiitake or maitake mushrooms.

**Makes 4 servings**

6 oz ground pork or chopped fresh mushrooms
2 tsp rice wine or dry sherry
1 tsp soy sauce
1 tsp peeled and minced fresh ginger
2 garlic cloves, chopped
2 Tbsp extra-virgin olive oil
1½ Tbsp Sichuan peppercorns, powdered or finely ground
3 Tbsp doubanjiang
1½ tsp cornstarch
1 cup rice milk or water
14 oz firm tofu, cut into ¾ in cubes
2 tsp chili oil
¼ tsp five-spice powder
1 green onion, minced
¼ tsp sesame oil
Steamed rice, for serving

# HOW TO MAKE OLD POCKMARKED LADY'S MAPO TOFU

In a medium bowl, combine the pork, rice wine, soy sauce, ginger, and garlic. Mix well.

In a large nonstick skillet over medium-high heat, heat the olive oil.

Add the pork mixture, Sichuan peppercorns, and doubanjiang. Cook over medium heat and stir until the pork is evenly coated with doubanjiang and cooked through.

Meanwhile, in a small bowl, whisk the cornstarch with the rice milk.

Spread the tofu evenly on top of the ground pork.

Add the cornstarch mixture, chili oil, and five-spice powder.

Use a spatula to gently toss the tofu with the meat mixture.

Bring the mixture to a boil, reduce to a simmer, and cook until the sauce thickens, about 5 minutes.

Garnish with green onion and drizzled sesame oil, and serve hot over steamed rice.

To store, seal leftover tofu in an airtight container and refrigerate for up to 3 days.

# RAGING STEAMED MEAT WITH RICE POWDER

During the Song dynasty, in 1003, Magistrate Huang lived in the Sichuan province. He embezzled money, pocketed taxes, and was quick to anger. Anyone who spoke out against him was jailed under false charges.

Every morning, Magistrate Huang would visit a cafe named Dine and Dash and order a big plate of steamed meat buns, deep-fried bread, a bowl of tofu curd, and anything else that he spotted. He would eat until he was full and leave without paying.

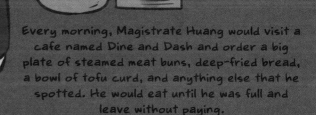

He is going to put us out of business!

Look at his big stomach! No wonder he needs me to make him a new robe every month. He never pays me either!

Every time I see him walking to the gambling mahjong den, I hide because I know he will ask me to loan him more jewelry that he'll just gamble away.

The townspeople hated the magistrate. But they knew better than to challenge him, for he could land them in jail . . . or worse.

One day, after the magistrate ate another unpaid meal, he complained to Chef Wang that the peanuts were not crispy and the tofu was sour.

Enraged, Chef Wang ran into the kitchen and threw a piece of fat pork belly onto the cutting board. He imagined the piece of meat was the magistrate and immersed it in spicy chiles, ginger, and soy sauce.

The next morning he wrapped it with thin noodles, imagining they were ropes tied around the magistrate. He then steamed the meat on high heat, fantasizing that he was cooking Magistrate Huang!

The next day, Chef Wang put up a sign.

NEW MENU SPECIAL!
RAGING STEAMED MEAT

Bring me the special. Let's see if Chef Wang has finally come up with something that's edible.

Afraid the magistrate would notice the imaginary ropes, Chef Wang quickly coated the noodle-wrapped meat with rice powder.

This is the best dish you've ever made! Bring me another to take home!

When the magistrate finally left, Chef Wang whispered the inspiration for his new dish to his regular customers. They were excited to tell their family and friends about the new dish.

When news spread about the hidden meaning of "raging steamed meat," Chef Wang's small restaurant overflowed with customers—not just for its food, but to vent their frustrations.

Every time Magistrate Huang visited the restaurant, he could hear laughter from the streets. But upon the magistrate's entrance, silence fell. He surmised that the taunting stares and stifled laughter were directed at him.

HAHA HAHA

One day, he decided to eavesdrop outside the restaurant.

HAHA

Yeah, Magistrate Huang is the only one who doesn't know the meaning of this dish in town!

Chef Wang, did you see how Magistrate Huang's tummy has grown even bigger? He demanded that I make him another outfit yesterday! Could you find a piece of pork belly as fat as his?

For that, I would first need to find longer noodles to tie the fat pig! Maybe then he would not walk around town guilting us for free food, and would be paying for his gambling debts and clothes!

HAHA HAHA HAHA

That night, many townspeople claimed to have heard shouting and stomping coming from the direction of the magistrate's office. The next day, Magistrate Huang was found dead. The town doctor declared he died from a fit of anger.

From that day on, Chef Wang coated the meat only in rice powder, for he no longer needed to wrap noodle "ropes" around the pork belly. It was then that he changed the dish's name to "raging steamed meat with rice powder."

# RAGING STEAMED MEAT WITH RICE POWDER （怒蒸粉蒸肉）

This dish, fen zheng rou, has many different varieties and flavors. The seasoned rice powder is what makes it special. To save time, you can buy pre-packaged rice powder at your local Asian grocery or online. You can also substitute the pork belly with beef. Be creative with your ingredients and you may be delighted with a pig-ture perfect dish!

**Makes 4 servings**

1 lb pork belly, rinsed, dried, and sliced into ¼ in thick pieces
1 tsp peeled and minced fresh ginger
2 tsp rice wine
1 Tbsp doubanjiang
1 tsp five-spice powder
½ tsp granulated sugar
¾ cup short-grain rice
½ cup sweet rice
1 tsp fennel seeds
1 star anise
1 bay leaf
8 Sichuan peppercorns
½ tsp salt
½ tsp ground white pepper
2 medium sweet potatoes, cut into 3 in cubes
2 tsp soy sauce
1 green onion, green parts only, minced

# HOW TO MAKE RAGING STEAMED MEAT WITH RICE POWDER

To marinate the pork belly, in a large bowl, mix the sliced pork belly with the ginger, rice wine, doubanjiang, five-spice powder, and sugar.

Cover and marinate for 2 hours or up to overnight in the refrigerator.

To make the rice powder, in a wok over medium-low heat, combine the short-grain rice, sweet rice, fennel, star anise, bay leaf, peppercorns, salt, and pepper.

Cook and stir until the rice turns light brown, about 5 minutes.

Remove from the heat and let the mixture cool.

Place the rice mixture in a food processor or mortar and pulverize it into a coarse grinded powder.

Stir in ½ cup water to create a thick paste.

Coat the pork belly with the paste.

In a heat-resistant bowl, mix the sweet potatoes with the soy sauce and lay an even layer on the bottom of the bowl.

Place the pork slices evenly on top of the potatoes.

Place the assembled dish in a steamer and cover it tightly.

Bring the steamer's water to a boil over high heat, then lower the heat to medium-high.

Steam for 1½ hours, periodically checking to make sure the steamer has enough water.

When done, garnish with green onions and serve hot.

To store, seal leftovers in an airtight container and refrigerate for up to 5 days.

# TWICE-COOKED PORK

The village of Le Le, or "Joy," in the mountainous Sichuan province was so remote that government officials rarely visited, and they often forgot to collect annual taxes from the villagers. The elders in Le Le Village greeted each other with the saying, "The sky is far away, and the emperor even farther." Children greeted each other with, "There is no tiger in the mountain! We monkeys are kings."

Everyone lived in tranquility in Le Le until one terrible fall morning. When the villagers opened their doors and windows to let in the morning sun, they saw millions of black locusts bearing down upon their fields. In less than a day, the horrible insects devoured all their crops!

Weeks later, word arrived that the third emperor of the Qing dynasty (1644–1911), Emperor Qianlong, was on his way to Le Le Village.

Qianlong was famous for his "dining tours." Every fall, he traveled all around China, seeking new exotic dishes to satisfy his gourmet appetite. At every stop, he demanded a feast. It was said that if he wasn't pleased, his anger was terrifying.

By the time the emperor was scheduled to arrive, the villagers had barely enough food for themselves, much less for an elaborate banquet for the emperor.

The leaders of Le Le met and decided that the only solution was to require every family to contribute one dish to the feast. They prayed to the kitchen god and the Emperor of Heaven that it would be enough to satisfy their gourmand emperor.

When the Kangs received the order, Mom and Pop Kang and their hungry boy, Ming, were just about to eat their dinner—a thin soup of pork and vegetables.

Where can we find food to make a dish? I just boiled our last bits of meat.

I wish we hadn't slaughtered the pig. Well, I'll see what I can find in the woods.

I will try to borrow some rice from the neighbors.

Ming watched his worried parents scuffling out the door. He decided he had to help.

After staring at the pieces of meat in his bowl for a while, an idea came to him.

With his chopsticks, he fished out all the meat from the pot and put them into his bowl.

He then went to their empty garden. Using a shovel, he dug and dug. Despite his best efforts, he found only a muddy onion and a few small carrots.

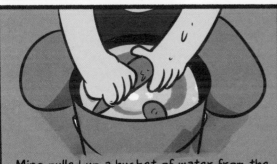
Ming pulled up a bucket of water from the well. He carefully washed and scrubbed the vegetables and cut them into small chunks.

Then he heated up some oil in a wok. When the oil started sizzling, he dropped in some minced garlic and chiles. The aroma filled their little room.

Ming dropped in the meat chunks he had taken from the soup and stir-fried them. A few minutes later, he stirred in the vegetables and a big spoonful of Momma Kang's special sauce.

When the vegetables and the boiled meat were coated with the dark brown sauce, he removed them from the wok and put them into a bowl decorated with the Chinese character "Double Happy."

Mom and Pop came home empty-handed and worried. They were astonished and delighted to see Ming's brilliant revival of their leftover meat!

The Kang family presented Ming's dish to the emperor as "twice-cooked pork." The unusual name and pungent smell immediately captivated the emperor. The emperor fell in love with it and devoured it hungrily.

From that day on, twice-cooked pork became a popular dish in the capital of the Sichuan province and, ultimately, across the globe.

# TWICE-COOKED PORK
## (回锅肉)

Just like Ming (page 89), be creative with your cooking of this dish! You can use just about any vegetables that you like and are in season and adjust the spiciness to your taste. Whether a prestigious emperor or a hungry houseguest, everyone will be enchanted by the deliciousness of this savory meal.

**Makes 4 servings**

1 lb lean pork loin or pork butt
4 slices peeled fresh ginger
1 Tbsp rice wine or dry sherry
2 Tbsp soy sauce
2 Tbsp extra-virgin olive oil
1 jalapeño, seeded and minced
3 green onions, cut into 2 in slices
1 red bell pepper, cut into chunks
2 Tbsp chili paste
Steamed rice or noodles, for serving

# HOW TO MAKE TWICE-COOKED PORK

In a large saucepan, cover the pork with cold water.

Add the ginger and bring to a boil over high heat.

Reduce the heat to medium-high, and cook the pork for 20 minutes.

Drain the pork and let it cool.

Slice the pork, cutting across the grain, into thin slices about 2 in long.

In a large bowl, combine the rice wine and soy sauce.

Marinate the pork in the mixture for approximately 30 minutes.

In a wok or cast-iron pan, heat the oil over medium-high heat.

Add the jalapeño and green onions.

Cook and stir for 1 minute and then add the red peppers.

Stir until the peppers are tender, about 1 minute.

Add the pork and marinade, and the chilli paste. Reduce the heat to low.

Cook and stir for 2 minutes. Serve hot with rice or noodles.

To store, seal leftovers in an airtight container and refrigerate for up to 3 days.

# ANTS CLIMBING A TREE

Have you ever seen the dish "ants climbing a tree" on a Chinese menu? Were you tempted to order it just to know what cooked ants taste like? Despite the name, you won't find ants in this dish.

When I was a little girl, dinner was a race to the table between my two older brothers and me. To make sure I got my fair share, Nai Nai always served me the first bowl.

The first time Nai Nai made ants climbing a tree, she said excitedly, "I hope you all like my new dish: ants climbing a tree."

My brothers hovered over the dish and marveled.

Wow, are they real ants?

Of course not! Thos are minced meat.

Haha!

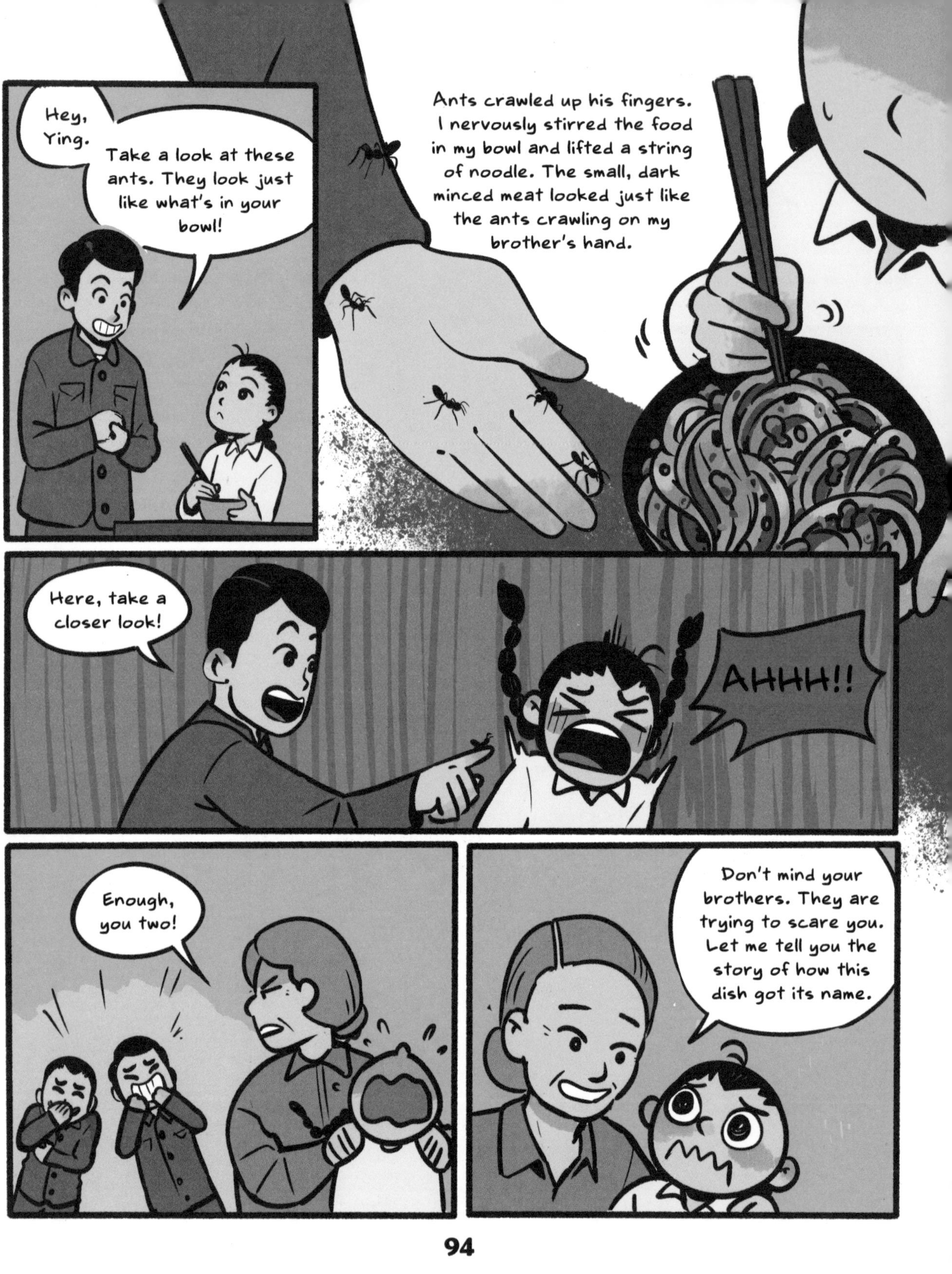
Hey, Ying.
Take a look at these ants. They look just like what's in your bowl!
Ants crawled up his fingers. I nervously stirred the food in my bowl and lifted a string of noodle. The small, dark minced meat looked just like the ants crawling on my brother's hand.
Here, take a closer look!
AHHH!!
Enough, you two!
Don't mind your brothers. They are trying to scare you. Let me tell you the story of how this dish got its name.

Long ago, there was a famous playwright, Guan Hanqing, from the Yuan dynasty (1271–1368). He wrote a story about a young, poor widowed woman named Dou E, who lived in a small village in Jiangsu province.

Dou E had to tend to her sick mother-in-law. She used whatever money she could muster to make nutritious dishes for the elderly woman.

One day, Dou E went to the butcher and hoped to buy a small piece of meat on credit.

Sir, could you please sell me some meat today? My mother-in-law hasn't eaten meat for weeks. I will pay you as soon as I can.

Although she hadn't paid off her last debt, the butcher was moved by Dou E's filial piety toward her mother-in-law. He cut off a small piece of pork for her.

When Dou E got home, she looked at the tiny piece of meat and thought long and hard about how she could stretch her ingredients to make a delicious and nutritious dish. After a while, an idea came.

She dropped a bundle of mung bean glass noodles into a hot pot of water.

Once the noodles softened, she drained and set the noodles aside.

Then she minced the pork into small pieces and flavored it with spices.

She heated oil in a wok and stir-fried the meat mixture. She then added chopped fresh garlic and ginger.

Dou E then stirred in spicy fermented bean sauce, finely chopped green onion, cilantro, bird's-eye chile, ground white pepper, and Shaoxing wine.

At last she dropped in the noodles and stir-fried them until they were coated with the meat and sauce.

Dou E served the dish to her mother-in-law.

The mother-in-law took a long look at the dish before her.

Dou E knew her mother-in-law's poor eyesight was playing tricks on her, and she gently explained what was in the dish.

Are those ants climbing on a tree?

Dou E waited nervously. The old woman took one bite...

...and then another.

Then her mother-in-law burst out crying.

It's so soft and flavorful! It's delicious!

Before long, ants climbing a tree became the talk of the village. Every family made it!

So now you know, there were never any ants in the dish.

Still, for a long time, whenever Nai Nai served the dish, my brothers would tease me about the ants in my bowl. With a grin, I would pick up a piece of small meat and say, "Mmmmm, I love eating ants. They're so soft and flavorful! They're delicious!"

# ANTS CLIMBING A TREE
## （蚂蚁上树）

Don't worry, this dish is neither creepy nor crawly. It gets its unappealing name from its appearance, not its ingredients. You can use either sweet potato or mung bean glass noodles. It tastes even better the next day, cold or warm.

**Makes 4 servings**

12 oz minced beef or pork
1½ tsp five-spice powder
1 Tbsp hoisin sauce
14 oz glass noodles
1½ tsp sesame oil
2 Tbsp extra-virgin olive oil
2 Tbsp doubanjiang
2 tsp peeled and minced fresh ginger
3 garlic cloves, minced
2 Tbsp soy sauce
1½ cups vegetable stock or water
1 green onion, green parts only, chopped

# HOW TO MAKE ANTS CLIMBING A TREE

To prepare the meat, in a medium bowl, mix the minced beef with the five-spice powder and hoisin sauce.

Cover and refrigerate for 1 hour.

To prepare the noodles, soak them in warm water for 10 minutes or until soft.

Drain and set aside.

Toss with the sesame oil to prevent sticking.

In a wok over medium heat, heat the olive oil.

Cook the beef mixture until aromatic and crispy.

Add the doubanjiang, ginger, and garlic and stir-fry for 2 minutes.

Add the softened noodles, soy sauce, and vegetable stock and stir.

When most of the stock is absorbed by the noodles, sprinkle the green onions on top of the noodles and serve hot.

To store, seal leftovers in an airtight container and refrigerate for up to 3 days.

# MONGOLIAN BEEF

Would you be surprised if I told you that Mongolian beef has nothing to do with Mongolia?

To learn the origins of the dish, you must meet Wu Jau-nan, a Chinese chef who later became a comedian.

Mr. Wu was born in Beijing on January 14, 1926. After the Communist Party took over China, he fled to Taiwan in 1949.

Noticing the barbecue trend, he opened a food stall on Yingqiao Street in Taipei.

Inspired by his hometown, Mr. Wu created a recipe with tender flank steak, onions, green onions, and vegetables in a dark, sweet, savory sauce. He wanted to name it Beijing Barbecue, but when Beijing became the capital of the People's Republic of China, he chose a different name.

As in Mongolian cooking, Wu used a lot of meat and onions, and cooked quickly over high heat. He named his dish Mongolian beef.

Wu was not only a good chef, but he also had a friendly and funny personality. In his spare time, he studied Xiangsheng, a traditional, popular performing art in Chinese comedy dialogue.

Customers enjoyed Wu's food as much as his jokes. His Mongolian beef quickly became popular all over Taiwan, and other chefs began to duplicate his dishes. Years later, Wu decided to pursue his passion for Xiangsheng. He closed his restaurant and devoted his time to perfecting his acting skills-ultimately becoming one of the most famous Xiangsheng actors in Taiwan. But most people still remember him as the creator of the world-famous Mongolian beef.

# MONGOLIAN BEEF
## （蒙古牛）

Mongolian beef has become an incredibly popular dish, especially in Chinese restaurants in the United States. Although it was created by a Beijing chef in Taiwan, it's an adaptation of Mongolian cooking, hence its contradictory name. While this iconic dish is usually cooked with onions, you can also add seasonal vegetables to your liking.

**Makes 4 servings**

1 tsp sesame oil
1 Tbsp rice vinegar
3 Tbsp orange juice
1 Tbsp oyster sauce
⅛ tsp red pepper flakes
¼ tsp sea salt
1 Tbsp soy sauce
1½ tsp rice wine or dry sherry
1½ tsp lemon juice
1 lb flank steak, thinly sliced against the grain
2 Tbsp extra-virgin olive oil
1 Tbsp peeled and minced fresh ginger
3 Tbsp minced orange peel
¼ cup sliced onion
2 green onions, cut into 1 in diagonal slices
Steamed rice or cooked noodles, for serving

# HOW TO MAKE MONGOLIAN BEEF

To make the sauce, in a small bowl, combine the sesame oil, rice vinegar, orange juice, oyster sauce, red pepper flakes, and salt.

Cover and set aside.

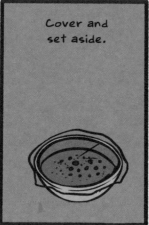

To prepare the meat, in a medium bowl, combine the soy sauce, rice wine, lemon juice, and flank steak. Set aside to marinate for 15 minutes.

In a large nonstick skillet over medium-high heat, heat the olive oil until it is hot.

Add the ginger and the orange peel and sauté until the ginger turns brown.

Add the marinated steak and stir-fry for about 2 minutes.

Add the onion and green onions and stir-fry for 1 minute.

Add the sauce and cook, stirring, until heated through, about 1 minute.

Serve over steamed rice or noodles.

To store, seal leftovers in an airtight container and refrigerate for up to 3 days.

# CHOP SUEY

There are many tales about the origin of chop suey, but no one knows which one is accurate. The most popular one is about an angry Chinese chef in California.

The legend says that during the Gold Rush in the 1850s, tension brewed between Americans and the influx of migrant Chinese workers.

One late, chilly night, a group of American miners banged on the door of Red Lantern, a Chinese restaurant.

Cook something for us. We are starving!

We have sold out of our food today said the chef. Please leave.

We will trash this place if you don't serve us!

The angry chef sized up the big, hungry workers and decided it was not worth fighting with them. So he stormed into the kitchen.

The counter was filled with scraps of old carrots, wilted cabbage, and a bag of chicken gizzards, pork livers, and calf's tripe.

The chef filled a big pot with water and dumped in the scraps.

Once it came to a boil, he seasoned it with soy sauce, rice wine, and salt and pepper and served it to the miners.

To his surprise, the miners loved the stew and finished every last bit!

Oh, this is just what I need on a cold night!

This is the best dish I have had in a long time. What's the name of it?

Um... Tsap Seui.

What the miners didn't know was that "Tsap seui" means "miscellaneous leftovers" in Chinese.

Never heard of it, but we are coming back for more!

Next day, the miners told all their friends about the savory dish they ate, but they mispronounced it as "chop suey." From then on, people came to Red Lantern asking for chop suey. Before long, "miscellaneous leftovers" became one of the most sought-after Chinese restaurant dishes.

These days, chefs rarely use leftover or assorted animal parts to create the dish. The modern recipe, which is much more appetizing, includes fresh seafood, pork, or chicken and vegetables with various seasonings.

# CHOP SUEY
## (什锦杂炒)

Do you have too many vegetables lying around? Want to try a one-dish meal? Then whip them into this iconic Chinese dish! The soul of chop suey lies in its exceptional sauce. Be creative and have fun matching your favorite ingredients together. You can swap out the shrimp for chicken or beef, use other veggies, or adjust the sauce. For vegetarians, replace the meat with firm tofu. Have fun!

**Makes 4 servings**

**Sauce**

1 cup vegetable stock or rice milk

2 Tbsp hoisin sauce

2 Tbsp soy sauce

1 Tbsp peeled and minced fresh ginger

2 garlic cloves, minced

1 Tbsp cornstarch

1 tsp sesame oil

¼ tsp red pepper flakes

**Chop Suey**

2 Tbsp extra-virgin olive oil

1 lb shrimp, peeled and deveined

8 oz bok choy, washed and cut into 3 in ribbons

½ cup thinly sliced red bell pepper

8 oz bean sprouts

Steamed rice, for serving

# HOW TO MAKE CHOP SUEY

To make the sauce, in a medium bowl, whisk together all the sauce ingredients. Set aside.

To make the chop suey, in a large skillet or wok over medium-high heat, heat the olive oil.

Add the shrimp and sauté for 1 minute.

Add the bok choy and bell pepper and stir-fry until the vegetables are almost tender, about 2 minutes.

Stir in the sauce. Add the bean sprouts.

Stir until everything is mixed and heated through.

Serve with rice.

To store, seal leftovers in an airtight container and refrigerate for up to 3 days.

# EDAMAME AND WORMS

Growing up in China during the Cultural Revolution (1966-1976), meat was rationed, so my family and I lived on a plant-based diet. Soybeans are a great source of protein and thus were a staple in Nai Nai's cooking.

In the mornings, I often accompanied her to the vegetable markets.

Whenever she bought edamame, I knew she would make my favorite dish: stir-fried spicy edamame.

While I loved eating the soybeans, I hated separating the slippery green beans from their furry pods. My two older brothers always found excuses for why they couldn't help, so the task fell to me.

One day, I was sitting under the big maidenhair tree in front of our home, shelling a small basket full of edamame pods into a bowl.

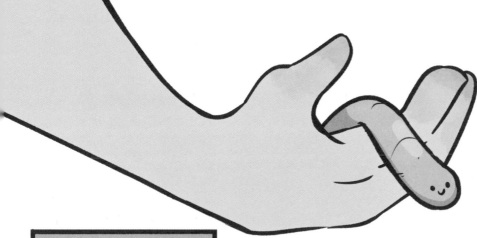

Suddenly I felt
something soft
squirming in my hand.
It was a big, green,
chubby worm.

Worm! Worm!
There is a
worm inside
the pot!

It won't hurt
you. It's
harmless.

I went back and squatted
near the wiggly worm.
It looked adorable.

So I went into the house and found a small jar to house it. I covered the top with paper and used chopsticks to poke three airholes in it.

I took it to my brothers and a group of neighborhood boys who were playing marbles in the courtyard.

Look what I have!

Let me see.

No, it's mine!

Where did you get it?

Inside the edamame.

I want one!

Oh, there are more in that pile of edamame.

The boys grabbed a handful of pods and got to work. While none of them came across any worms, they helped me shell the rest of the soybeans!

Unfortunately, the next time Nai Nai assigned me to shell the beans, I couldn't trick the boys to help.

Years later, when I came to the United States, I saw bags of shelled frozen edamame in the grocery store. I was elated by the convenience, which reminded me of my childhood!

FROZEN EDAMAME

# STIR-FRIED EDAMAME WITH CHILES AND TOFU （辣椒豆腐炒毛豆）

When I was young, millions of Chinese people thrived on protein-rich, soy-based foods because meat was strictly rationed. Chinese medicine doctors consider soy yin, or cooling. They prescribe it to treat fevers, headaches, chest distention, and hyperactivity, as well as a tonic for the lungs and stomach. Cranberries are a good source of ellagic acid, an antioxidant compound. So this healing dish is one of my favorites!

**Makes 4 servings**

1 Tbsp extra-virgin olive oil

2 tsp fresh minced chile

One 7 oz packet Teriyaki Baked Tofu, cut into 1 in cubes

2 cups shelled frozen edamame

1 medium leek (about 8 oz), white part only, thinly sliced

½ cup dried cranberries

1 Tbsp soy sauce

1 Tbsp rice vinegar

2 tsp sesame oil

¼ cup pine nuts, toasted

# HOW TO MAKE STIR-FRIED EDAMAME WITH CHILES AND TOFU

Heat a wok or nonstick skillet over medium-high heat.

Add the olive oil and swirl to coat.

Add the chile and tofu and stir-fry until golden brown, about 2 minutes.

Add the edamame and stir-fry for 2 minutes or until heated through.

Add the leek, cranberries, soy sauce, and rice vinegar and stir-fry until the leek is soft, 1 to 2 minutes.

RICE VINEGAR

SOY SAUCE

Transfer the tofu mixture to a serving dish and drizzle with the sesame oil.

麻油 SESAME OIL

Garnish with the toasted pine nuts and serve hot.

To store, seal leftovers in an airtight container and refrigerate for up to 3 days.

# THE YOUNGEST PRIME MINISTER

In 475 BC, seven states occupied China: Chu, Han, Qi, Qin, Wei, Yan, and Zhao. They were constantly fighting for territory and power. King Qin had launched a war against Zhao, but his army made very slow progress in conquering their territory. The delays made him furious.

One cold, rainy day, Minister Mao left the Qin court after sunset. His teenage son, Gan Lou, always waiting for him, ran up to him, enjoying their walks and court stories.

So, who did the king make a fool of today?

A poor farmer claimed he found a way to speed up seedling growth. Today, he came to court crying—they had all died because he had been pulling on them!

HAHA!

Worry fell over Lou. The rest of the walk he thought long and hard . . . then an idea formed.

The next morning, Lou got up early. He ran to the chicken coop, gathered a handful of eggs, and picked a few bright orange and red tomatoes from the garden.

He cut the tomatoes into small pieces, beat the eggs, and flavored them with salt and pepper. He then heated oil in his wok and stir-fried the eggs with minced green onion.

He stirred in the diced tomatoes and seasoned them with soy sauce and sesame oil.

The delicious aroma woke his parents.

What are you doing?

I cooked the egg dish for King Qin. I am going to court in your place.

Lou put the egg dish in a wooden box decorated with a hen and a flock of chicks. Before his parents could protest, Lou put on his father's hat and robe and hurried out the door.

When Gan Lou waltzed into court, the hat slipped below his eyes, and the robe pooled around his feet. All eyes fell on him. He walked toward King Qin, trying not to trip.

Who are you? What is this?

I am Minister Mao's son, and this is a dish cooked with rooster eggs.

Where is your father?

Oh, your honor, my father is at home, giving birth to a baby.

Giggles broke out around the court.

What nonsense! How can a man give birth to a child?

The court fell silent. All the ministers held their breath.

Well, your Majesty, if you don't believe a man can give birth to a child, then why do you believe a rooster can lay eggs?

The king's face reddened. He snatched the box.

When he opened it, the delicious smell swirled through the court.

Mmmm, it's a very colorful dish . . .

Mmmm, the tangy tomato complements the flavorful egg very nicely. Now go home and tell your father to come to my court with you tomorrow!

Lou rushed out and found his worried father waiting outside.

When Lou told his father what had happened, his father hugged him tightly.

The next day, when they went to court, the king appointed twelve-year-old Lou to be his father's assistant!

Eventually, Gan Lou became the youngest prime minister of the Qin court, and King Qin unified the Warring States to become the first emperor of China. To show his appreciation for Lou's bold sense of humor and great cooking skills, King Qin made the stir-fried tomato and egg dish one of his banquets' signature dishes!

# STIR-FRIED ROOSTER EGGS WITH TOMATOES （西红柿炒鸡蛋）

This extremely popular dish is a comfort food for any Chinese person far from home. Scrambled eggs and fresh tomatoes work together to create a plethora of salty, sour, and sweet flavors.

## Makes 4 servings

3 medium tomatoes
5 eggs
¼ tsp sea salt
¼ tsp ground white pepper
½ tsp sesame oil
3 Tbsp extra-virgin olive oil
3 garlic cloves, minced
1 Tbsp soy sauce
3 green onions, minced
Cooked white rice or noodles, for serving

# HOW TO MAKE STIR-FRIED ROOSTER EGGS WITH TOMATOES

Cut each tomato into 4 wedges.

In a medium bowl, beat the eggs, salt, pepper, and sesame oil until smooth. Set aside.

In a wok over medium-high heat, heat 2 Tbsp of the olive oil.

Add the eggs and cook, stirring lightly, until set.

Remove the eggs and set aside.

Heat the remaining 1 Tbsp of olive oil in the wok.

Add the garlic and stir until fragrant, about 20 seconds.

Add the tomatoes and the soy sauce.

Stir in the cooked eggs.

Cook and stir until the tomato flesh has softened and begun to form a sauce, about 2 minutes.

Garnish with the green onions and serve warm with rice or noodles.

123

To store, seal leftovers in an airtight container and refrigerate for up to 3 days.

# FORBIDDEN RICE WITH EGGS AND ALMONDS

You may have read about the health benefits of black rice in recent years. But have you heard how this healthy rice got the name "forbidden rice"?

This rice has a deep, black color, a delicious nutty taste, and a soft texture.

Legend has it that 10,000 years ago, during the Song dynasty (960-1279), a very dark-colored strain of rice originated from a crop in China.

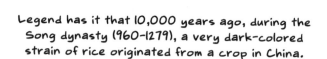

Because this exotic grain had a much lower yield than other kinds of rice, it was reserved for only the emperor and the royal family. Anyone who ate it without the emperor's permission could face harsh punishment—even death. Henceforth, it got its name: forbidden rice.

Luckily black rice is widely available online, at natural food stores and Asian markets, so everyone can enjoy it.

# Interesting facts about forbidden rice:

It contains more than 23 antioxidants and has the highest antioxidant activity of all rice varieties.

According to traditional Chinese medicine, black rice is considered neutral, so it can be consumed in all seasons.

Chinese medicine doctors believe it helps to replenish one's qi, or vital energy.

It's also referred to as longevity rice, as it's believed to free one from physical or mental sickness.

It is gluten-free, so it's a good option for those who have gluten sensitivity and offers a good source of protein, fiber, and iron.

# FORBIDDEN RICE WITH EGGS AND ALMONDS (鸡蛋杏仁黑米禁饭)

Like brown rice, forbidden rice requires a little more water and time to cook than white rice. In this dish, the black rice, red cranberries, and colorful vegetables make a pleasing contrast that will cheer your spirits and brighten your table!

## Makes 4 servings

2 large eggs, lightly beaten

1½ tsp soy sauce, plus more as needed

2 tsp sesame oil

1 green onion, sliced, plus 2 green onions, white parts only, sliced

1 Tbsp olive oil

4 oz ham, cut into ½ in cubes

2 oz fresh shiitake mushrooms, stemmed, caps cut into 1 in wide slices

¼ cup green peas, fresh or frozen

1½ cups cooked black rice

¼ cup toasted almonds

¼ cup dried cranberries

# HOW TO MAKE FORBIDDEN RICE WITH EGGS AND ALMONDS

In a medium bowl, beat together the eggs, soy sauce, and sesame oil until well blended.

Stir in the green onion and set aside.

In a nonstick sauté pan over medium-high heat, heat the olive oil and swirl to coat.

Pour in the egg mixture.

Cook, without stirring, until the egg is softly set.

Break up the egg with a spatula.

Add the ham, shiitake mushrooms, peas, and cooked rice.

Cook, stirring, until the rice mixture is heated through.

Season with additional soy sauce to taste.

Garnish with the sliced green onion whites, almonds, and cranberries. Serve hot.

To store, seal leftover rice in an airtight container and refrigerate for up to 3 days.

# HEARTBREAK JELLY NOODLES

Heartbreak jelly noodles, or "tears of joy jelly," is a famous noodle dish from Sichuan known for its spicy and refreshing taste. The opaque white noodles are also called *liang fen*, which means "cold noodles" in Chinese. They are often made from mung beans or pea starch, giving them a jelly-like silky, slippery, and springy texture.

But why "heartbreak"? It could be that the noodles alone have a plain taste, so they're often served with a tangy sauce so spicy that those who eat the dish would burst into tears. The more they eat, the sadder and more heartbroken they seem.

It is also believed that if you are truly heartbroken after eating this dish, your sadness will vanish.

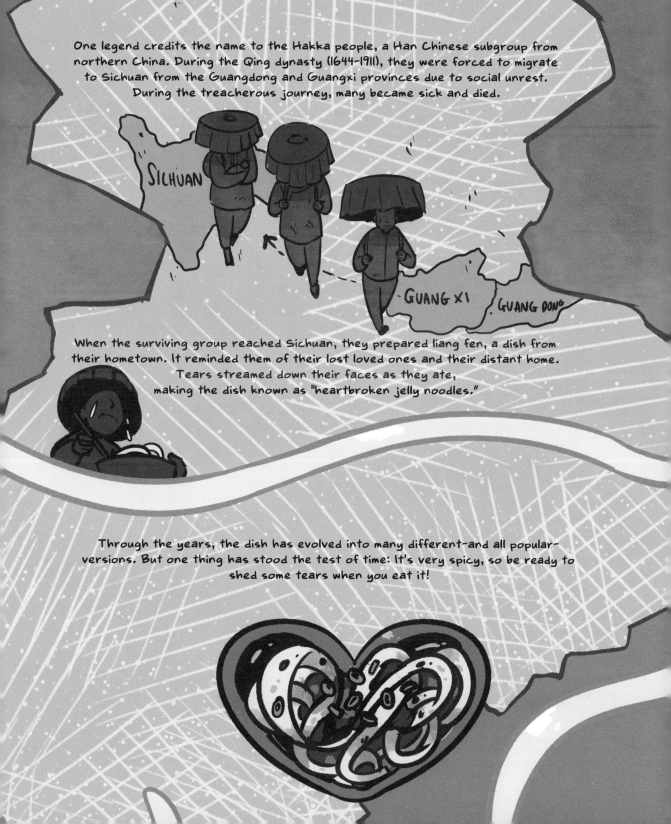

One legend credits the name to the Hakka people, a Han Chinese subgroup from northern China. During the Qing dynasty (1644-1911), they were forced to migrate to Sichuan from the Guangdong and Guangxi provinces due to social unrest. During the treacherous journey, many became sick and died.

SICHUAN

GUANG XI

GUANG DONG

When the surviving group reached Sichuan, they prepared liang fen, a dish from their hometown. It reminded them of their lost loved ones and their distant home. Tears streamed down their faces as they ate, making the dish known as "heartbroken jelly noodles."

Through the years, the dish has evolved into many different-and all popular- versions. But one thing has stood the test of time: It's very spicy, so be ready to shed some tears when you eat it!

# HEARTBREAK JELLY NOODLES
## （伤心凉粉）

The tear-inducing spiciness of this dish comes from a powerful combination of chili oil, peppercorns, and other fiery ingredients. Be sure to have a box of tissues nearby! Use high-quality chili oil to really enhance the spiciness. If you are not *that* heartbroken, you can use less red pepper and chili oil for a milder taste. Don't overwhelm the dish with spiciness, or else your tears will dilute the sauce!

**Makes 4 servings**

2 garlic cloves, minced
2 tsp red pepper flakes
¼ tsp Sichuan peppercorn powder
3 Tbsp extra-virgin olive oil
1 Tbsp chili oil
2 Tbsp black vinegar
2 Tbsp soy sauce
1 Tbsp sesame oil
½ tsp granulated sugar
¼ tsp sea salt
1 cup mung bean starch
1 green onion, green part only, minced
¼ cup peanuts, roasted or fried, smashed into small pieces

# HOW TO MAKE HEARTBREAK JELLY NOODLES

To make the sauce, in a medium bowl, combine the garlic, red pepper flakes, and Sichuan peppercorn powder.

In a small pot over medium-high heat, heat the olive oil and chili oil until hot.

Pour the hot oil over the garlic and chili mixture.

Mix in the black vinegar, soy sauce, sesame oil, sugar, and salt.

Cover and set aside.

To make the noodles, in a large bowl, whisk the mung bean starch with 1 cup of water until the starch is dissolved.

In a medium saucepan over high heat, bring 3½ cups of water to a boil.

Immediately turn the heat to medium-low and slowly pour in the mung bean starch while whisking quickly to prevent lumps.

Cook, whisking constantly, for about 2 minutes until the mixture thickens.

Pour the thick jelly into a 9 in square cake pan. Let it cool, about 30 minutes.

Cover and store in the fridge until it turns it into a firm jelly, about 1 hour.

Put one hand over the jelly to hold it against the pan, then flip the pan over a clean cutting board. The jelly will come out easily.

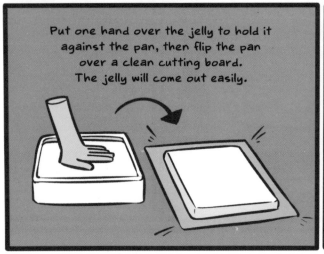

Cut the jelly into noodles about ½ in wide and 3 in long.

Arrange the noodles artistically in a serving bowl and pour the sauce over them.

Garnish with green onion and peanuts. Serve at room temperature or cold.

To store, seal leftovers in an airtight container and refrigerate for up to 3 days.

# BUDDHA JUMPS OVER THE WALL

Da was the youngest monk in the Xichan Temple, but he could out-eat all the other monk brothers. When they ventured into the Fuzhou district, the capital of Fujian province, locals would kneel before them and offer vegetarian food, as monks were forbidden to eat meat.

Da was always hungry no matter how much he ate, as if there were a hole inside him. His hunger intensified as days went by, and it became harder to focus on chanting. His mind wandered to the food he saw in the city.

GRUMBLE...

When Da caught himself daydreaming about chicken drumsticks, crispy shrimp, and beef noodles, he instantly felt guilty.

He prayed to the big Buddha statue in front of the temple.

Forgive me for my gluttonous mind. I will focus more on praying.

But soon, his thoughts were again overtaken by food. Goubuli baozi, dan dan noodles, and egg drop soup danced in his head.

One late afternoon, just when Da promised Buddha he would try harder to focus on his praying, a delicious, pungent scent wafted through the window. Da's mouth watered. He tried to ignore the smell, thinking his hunger must be so strong that he was imagining it.

Hmph. It's no matter. I will use chanting to clear my mind. I can do this.

The scent intensified. Da reached into his sleeves, where he normally kept a bun to calm his hunger, but it was empty. He chanted louder, hoping to chase away temptation.

A feathery cloud floated by, bearing the scent of roasted chicken, beef stew, and goubuli baozi. Sweat rolled down Da's back. Could no one else smell this delicious aroma? He opened his eyes and looked around. Other monks around him had their eyes shut tight, chanting under their breath.

Summoning his courage, Da slipped out into the hall. Despite the painted Buddhas staring at him from the ornate monastery wall, he followed an invisible force that seemed to be urging him forward.

When he realized the smell came from outside...

Da jumped over the wall.

On the other side he found an old man in a long scholar's robe, cooking something in a clay pot over an open fire.

Why are you cooking here? What are you cooking? Could I please have some?

I am a traveling scholar and I am making meat stew. I see you are in a monk's robe. This is not proper for you.

Don't think twice about it. I bet even Buddha himself would make an exception!

Feeling sorry for the hungry young monk, the scholar shared his meal with Da.

Thank you! I finally filled the hole inside of me!

When the scholar returned to his home city, he told people about his encounter with a hungry monk and named his dish "Buddha jumps over the wall."

# BUDDHA JUMPS OVER THE WALL（佛跳墙）

While in Asia, I loved visiting the elegant Buddhist temples. However, it wasn't for religious reasons—I simply enjoyed the food served in their dining halls. This recipe was inspired by a dish I ate at the Shaolin Temple. If you prefer a protein other than tofu, feel free to substitute it. The rich aroma of this tasty dish just may make your neighbors jump over the wall to beg for a taste!

## Makes 4 servings

Two 5 oz packages mung bean glass noodles
2 Tbsp extra-virgin olive oil
One 6 oz packet of savory baked tofu, cubed
½ cup coarsely chopped oyster mushrooms
4 oz baby corn
One 5 oz can water chestnuts, drained
2 Tbsp soy sauce
1½ tsp rice vinegar
1 Tbsp oyster sauce
2 tsp chili paste
¼ tsp sea salt
½ tsp freshly ground black pepper
½ tsp hot sesame oil
2 green onions, green parts only, minced

# HOW TO MAKE BUDDHA JUMPS OVER THE WALL

Soak the noodles in warm water for 10 minutes or until soft.

Drain and set aside.

In a large nonstick skillet over medium-high heat, heat the olive oil.

Stir-fry the tofu and mushrooms for 2 minutes.

Add the corn and water chestnuts. Stir-fry for 1 minute.

Add the soy sauce and rice vinegar.

Stir in the soft noodles, oyster sauce, chili paste, salt, and pepper.

Cover and let the noodles heat through, about 1 minute.

Transfer to a serving bowl.
Stir in the sesame oil and garnish with green onions.

To store, seal leftovers in an airtight container and refrigerate for up to 3 days.

Chapter 3

# Desse

# (甜點)

rts

# MOONCAKES

The Mid-Autumn Festival, also known as the Mooncake Festival, is widely regarded as one of the most important Chinese holidays.

On that evening, friends and family gather to marvel at the full moon, drink tea, and eat small wedges of mooncakes-round, small pastries that come with many different fillings, including sweet red bean paste, lotus root, nuts, or custard (as in my recipe, page 147).

Many legends and folktales are linked to mooncakes. In one of the most popular versions, ten suns took turns crossing the sky. Whenever they gathered, the oceans on earth boiled, the rivers evaporated, and the lakes dried out.

People kneeled under the shade of dying trees, threw their hands in the air, and pleaded to the suns to go away.

On the youngest sun's birthday, all the suns gathered for a party.
The people cried, "Please go home. You're burning us to death!"
"We are going to die from this heat!"
"You're killing our crops. We will have no food to eat!"

But the suns ignored their pleas and continued eating, drinking, and dancing.

Chang E, the wife of the powerful archer Huo Yi, asked her husband to save Earth. So Huo Yi took his biggest bow and ran to the top of the mountain.

Suns, please go back to your homes. We are suffering from your heat.

Haaaa! And what are you going to do if we don't?

Angry, Huo Yi drew his bow. His first arrow knocked over the suns' wine jar.

His next shot struck the eldest sun and turned him into a three-legged crow.

Huo Yi's wife and the villagers cheered and clapped. One by one, Huo Yi shot eight more suns, turning them all into crows.

The earth cooled down and people could breathe easily again.

Just one more sun left.

Leave that one, or we will be left in cold and darkness.

Huo Yi put down his bow. People rejoiced, lifted Huo Yi up in the air, and declared him their new king.

When the Queen of Heaven heard the news, she rewarded Huo Yi with a bottle of immortality elixir—which, if drunk, would make him ascend to the heavens and become a god.

But Huo Yi did not want to leave his beloved wife, Chang E, and relished in his newfound power on Earth.

As the years passed, Huo Yi grew into a ruthless, tyrannical ruler. He was harsh to his people and demanded they pay high taxes to fund the construction of his mansion. Anyone who dared to disagree with him was jailed.

When Chang E pleaded with her husband to be kinder, Huo Yi bantered and brushed her off.

As time went by, Chang E didn't want her cruel husband to drink the elixir and rule forever, so she hid the bottle in her rice jar.

Chang E became more and more unhappy. She spent her days in her kitchen full of dough, sugar, eggs, and red bean paste. Day and night, she baked sweet round cakes to give to people to comfort them.

That night, Chang E left a note to her once-beloved husband:

Dear husband,
You are not the man I married. I cannot stand it anymore. By the time you are reading this, I will be gone.

Your wife,
Chang E

He took up his bow and aimed it at Chang E. Ignoring her husband, Chang E continued ascending to the moon.

Come back, dear wife! Come back. I'm sorry!

I'm sorry, Chang E! Please come back! I will change—I will be a kinder ruler!

Despite Huo Yi's pleading, Chang E flew up into the clouds without looking back.

From that day on, the sorrowful Huo Yi became a gentle king.

To honor Chang E's kindness, people made her the Moon Goddess.

Since then, on the fifteenth day of the eighth lunar month, she is remembered during the Mid-Autumn Festival.

When the moon is full and bright, family and friends gather to honor the Moon Goddess by eating mooncakes. If you are lucky, on that night you will see Chang E's shadow on the moon.

And if you listen closely, you may even hear Huo Yi pleading for his wife's forgiveness.

Another famous mooncake legend involves Han Chinese rebel leader Zhu Yuanzhang and his advisor Liu Bo Wen. They used mooncakes to overthrow the Mongolian rulers.

To avoid Mongol spies, the rebels spread a rumor about a deadly plague and claimed special mooncakes could prevent it. Liu hid a secret message, "Uprising on the night of Mid-Autumn Festival," in the mooncakes and sent them to the resistance.

When Zhu's followers found the message in the mooncakes, they coordinated the uprising, overthrew the Mongols, and ended the Yuan dynasty (1271-1368). Zhu Yuanzhang then became the Hongwu Emperor and started the Ming dynasty (1368-1644).

# MOONCAKES
## (月饼)

Mooncakes are round pastries with various sweet fillings with tastes and styles unique to their regions. Traditional mooncake crust—made of flour, vegetable oil, and lard—is very labor intensive. However, making modern snow-skin mooncake crust is a much easier process and yields healthier results.

Note that for this recipe, you will need a mooncake mold.

**Makes 10 mooncakes**

**Filling**
4 oz butter, melted
½ cup milk powder
⅓ cup heavy cream
¼ cup wheat starch or tapioca starch
¼ cup granulated sugar

**Dough**
1 cup rice flour
1 cup glutinous rice flour
½ cup all-purpose flour
½ cup granulated sugar
½ cup heavy cream or whole milk
½ cup coconut oil
3 Tbsp beet juice or green tea powder (optional)
½ cup cornstarch

# HOW TO MAKE MOONCAKES

### FILLING

To make the filling, in a small pot over medium-low heat, combine the butter, milk powder, heavy cream, wheat starch, and sugar.

Cook, stirring, until it reduces into a thick paste.

Remove from the heat, let the mixture cool, and then form it into ten balls.

### DOUGH

To make the dough, in a large heatproof bowl, combine the rice flour, glutinous rice flour, all-purpose flour, and sugar.

In a separate bowl, combine the cream, oil, and beet juice (if using).

Make a well in the middle of the flour mixture.

Gradually add the wet mixture, stirring until a thin batter forms.

Transfer the mixture to a 10 in glass pie plate.

Bring the water to a boil over high heat in a covered steamer or pot large enough to hold the plate.

Cover and steam until translucent, about 20 minutes.

Let the dough cool to room temperature.

Once cooled, knead the dough into ten smooth balls.

To assemble, roll out each ball of dough to a 4 in round diameter, thick in the middle and thin around the edges.

Set one ball of filling in a dough's center and wrap it in the dough, gently pushing the wrapper upward to tightly cover the filling.

Seal at the top. Repeat with the remaining dough rounds.

Dust each assembled ball with cornstarch, shaking off any excess.

Place one ball into the mooncake mold.

Holding the mold with the opening facing down, gently press the springy handle to extract the mooncake onto a cornstarch dusted plate. Repeat with the remaining balls.

Serve at room temperature.

To store, seal leftovers in an airtight container and refrigerate for up to 3 days.

Mooncake molds are made of wood or plastic, and feature multiple designs. Look for 4 in molds that are 1 to 1½ in thick. They are available in many online stores.

If you don't have a mold, you can flatten the cake and decorate it with other designs you have on hand. Mooncakes taste best when served at room temperature. You can also store them in the freezer in a single layer. Once completely frozen, transfer them into airtight containers and freeze for up to 1 month.

# FORTUNE COOKIES

Did you know that fortune cookies, which are commonly served in Chinese restaurants in the West, are not originally from China but from America?

The exact origin of fortune cookies is still debated, as both Chinese and Japanese immigrant groups have insisted they should get credit for their popularity in the US in the twentieth century.

Here are some interesting facts about fortune cookies:

According to researcher Yasuko Nakamachi, the fortune cookie was likely invented by Japanese immigrants in California. When Japanese bakery owners were sent to internment camps during World War II, Chinese-owned manufacturers then took over.

In the early 1990s, Wonton Food Inc. tried to expand its US-based business into China. Their efforts failed, as many Chinese were so unaware of the cookies and their purpose that they inadvertently ate the paper fortunes!

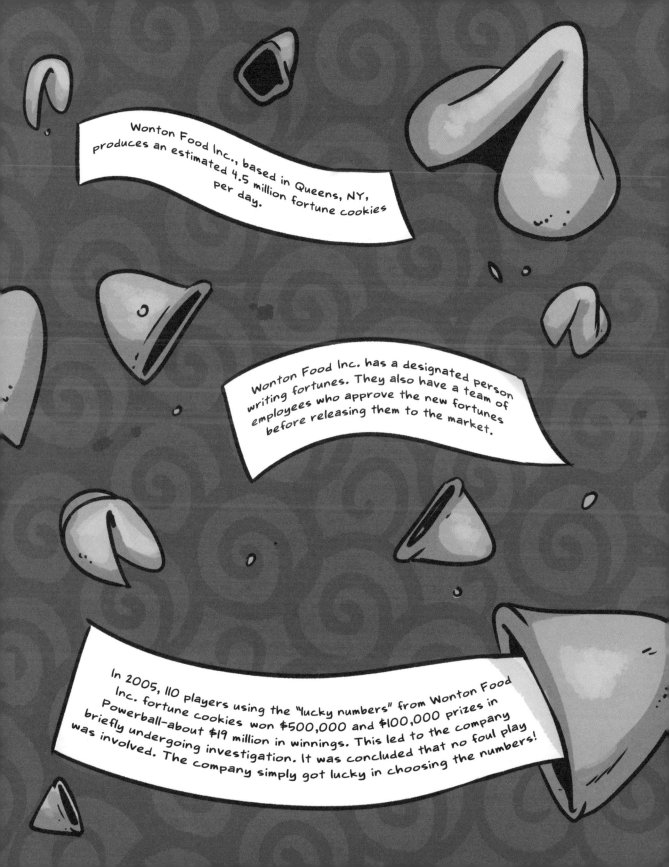

Wonton Food Inc., based in Queens, NY, produces an estimated 4.5 million fortune cookies per day.

Wonton Food Inc. has a designated person writing fortunes. They also have a team of employees who approve the new fortunes before releasing them to the market.

In 2005, 110 players using the "lucky numbers" from Wonton Food Inc. fortune cookies won $500,000 and $100,000 prizes in Powerball—about $19 million in winnings. This led to the company briefly undergoing investigation. It was concluded that no foul play was involved. The company simply got lucky in choosing the numbers!

# FORTUNE COOKIES
## （幸运饼干）

This crunchy cookie is an alluring delight in the West, being a ubiquitous treat in Chinese restaurants. Make sure the batter is thin and evenly spaced when baking. Wear gloves to protect your hands, and shape the cookies and insert your fortunes right after they're done baking. Don't be discouraged if your first try is not perfect—with patience, your cookies will be worth a "fortune!"

**Makes 10 cookies**

2 large egg whites
½ tsp vanilla extract
½ tsp almond extract
3 Tbsp butter, melted
¼ cup granulated sugar
½ cup all-purpose flour
1 Tbsp milk or water
¼ tsp sea salt

# HOW TO MAKE FORTUNE COOKIES

Cut ten strips of paper 3½ in long and ½ in wide. Write a fortune on each strip.

Preheat the oven to 300°F. Line a baking sheet with a silicone mat or parchment paper.

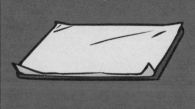

In a medium bowl, lightly beat the egg whites, vanilla extract, almond extract, and butter until frothy.

Add the sugar, flour, milk, and salt.

Whisk until the batter is smooth.

Scoop 1 Tbsp of batter at a time onto the prepared baking sheet, spacing the scoops 5 in apart.

Using the back of a spoon, press each scoop of batter into a 4 in round.

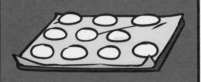

Bake until the edges seem crispy and golden brown and centers are still pale, about 10 minutes.

Use a spatula to lift the hot cookies out of the oven.

To shape a fortune cookie, place a fortune in the center and fold the cookie in half, pressing the edges together.

Gently pull the edges downward over a round handle of a wooden spoon to crease them into shape.

Repeat with all the cookies, working somewhat quickly before the cookies cool.

Repeat with the remaining batter.
Place the finished cookies in muffin-tin cups to hold their shape while they cool.

Once the cookies are completely cool and hard, remove them from the muffin tin and serve them at room temperature.

You may store them in a zipper bag or a sealed container for up to 1 week.

# ROCK SUGAR PEARS

When my son, Vinson, was young, I rarely allowed him to eat high-sugar foods. Whenever we went grocery shopping, he was always attracted to colorful candy bags and cereal boxes.

Mommy, can we buy this, please?

It's high in sugar. If you eat it, you will get confused.

Oh, I don't want to be confused!

Every night before bedtime, he would ask me to either read or tell him a story. His favorites were about my childhood growing up in Wuhan.

Can you tell me another story about my grandma?

I searched my brain for a story I had not yet told him. Then I remembered the tale of the rock sugar pears.

Do you remember how she was a Chinese doctor in Wuhan? When I had a cough, she would make me the best steamed pears stuffed with rock sugar.

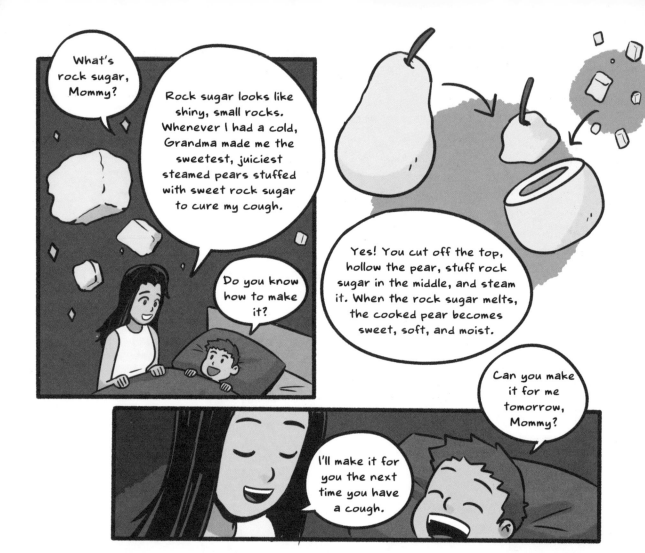

What's rock sugar, Mommy?

Rock sugar looks like shiny, small rocks. Whenever I had a cold, Grandma made me the sweetest, juiciest steamed pears stuffed with sweet rock sugar to cure my cough.

Do you know how to make it?

Yes! You cut off the top, hollow the pear, stuff rock sugar in the middle, and steam it. When the rock sugar melts, the cooked pear becomes sweet, soft, and moist.

Can you make it for me tomorrow, Mommy?

I'll make it for you the next time you have a cough.

The next day I was writing in my office when Vinson cracked the door open and stuck his little head inside.

Mommy, you have a message on your phone.

Puzzled, I checked my cell. There was a voice message from our home phone.

I broke into laughter and went into the kitchen, where I found Vinson already standing on his little cooking stool holding a pear.

He watched intently as I peeled and hollowed the pear, stuffing it with rock sugar.

He eagerly looked through the oven door, watching the sugar melt slowly inside the pear. That night, he ate a whole rock sugar pear for dessert.

From that day on, whenever Vinson was feeling under the weather (or was acting like it), we would make rock sugar pears together. Many years later, he told me that he makes this dish for himself at his own home—with or without coughing.

# ROCK SUGAR PEARS

## （冰糖梨）

Asian pears are also called apple pears because they are crisp, juicy, and round—just like apples. Traditional Chinese medicine doctors believe they have healing properties that soothe the lungs and throat. In this dish, the steaming pears absorb the sugar, becoming sweet and tender. If you don't have rock sugar, substitute honey.

**Makes 4 servings**

4 ripe Asian pears
¼ cup rock sugar, broken into very small pieces
Peeled and thinly sliced fresh ginger, for garnishing

# HOW TO MAKE ROCK SUGAR PEARS

In a steamer or wok large enough to hold a large steamer rack, bring water to a boil over high heat.

Peel the pears. Cut about ¼ of the top off and set aside.

Using a melon baller, working from the top of the pear, remove the core and seeds. Be careful not to cut through the bottoms of the pears.

Fill each hollowed-out pear with 1 Tbsp of rock sugar.

Arrange the pears upright in a large bowl and place the tops back on the pears.

Set the bowl on the steamer rack.

Cover the steamer and steam the pears until they are tender and the rock sugar has melted completely, 15 to 20 minutes.

Using oven mitts, carefully lift the steamer lid away from you and remove the bowl.

Transfer the pears to four smaller bowls.

Garnish each pear with the ginger slices. Serve hot.

To store, seal leftovers in an airtight container and refrigerate for up to 2 days.

# STEAMED MILK CUSTARD

Steamed milk custard is one of the most beloved desserts in China. The first time I tried it was at a tea house in Hong Kong. I later tried many other local variations, such as one topped with chopped fruit in Taiwan and another garnished with shaved fresh coconut in Thailand. Each time, I loved its creamy and silky texture.

Although there are several versions of its origin, all agree that the dish originated in the Guangzhou province as a way to preserve milk during the Qing dynasty (1644-1911).

According to one popular tale, a young cattle farmer named Dong and his father made a living raising cattle in Baishi Village, in the Shunde region of Guangdong. Every morning, the father and son would go to the market to sell milk.

By midday, unsold batches of milk would spoil, as there was no refrigeration then and the weather in Guangdong was always hot. The father and son made little money and were often hungry.

Day after day, Dong saw his dejected father pouring out batches of soon-to-be spoiled milk. He wished he could find a way to preserve it.

Wanting to help his father, one day, Dong took a jar of unsold milk home and boiled it.

Hours later, when the milk cooled, Dong was surprised to see a layer of white skin forming on the top.

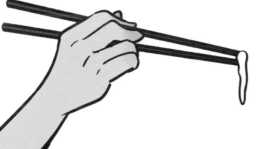

With the tips of his chopsticks, Dong gingerly lifted a small piece of skin and tasted it.

His eyes widened. Dong lifted a bigger piece and raced to his father.

Here! Here! Try this!

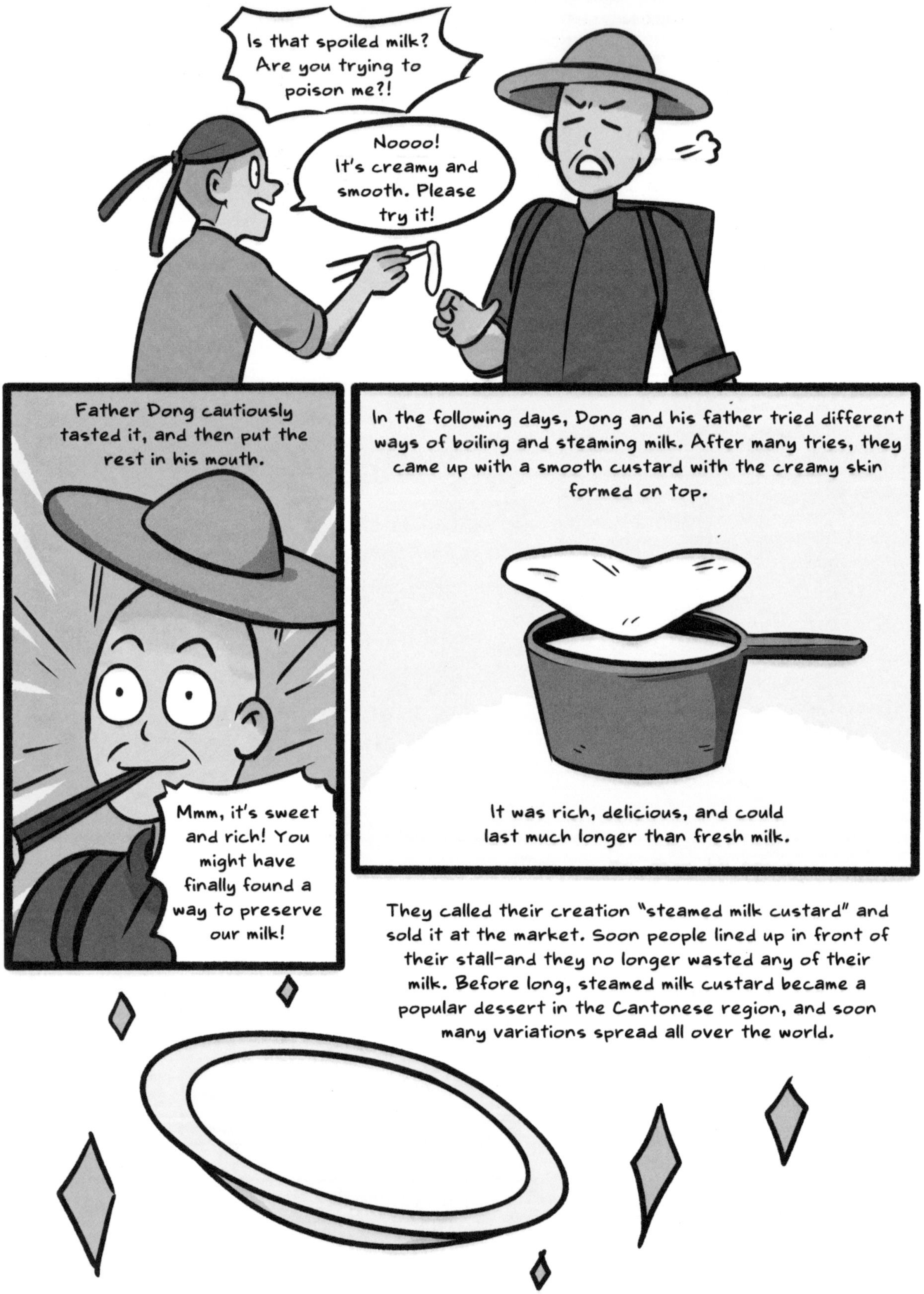
Is that spoiled milk? Are you trying to poison me?!
Noooo! It's creamy and smooth. Please try it!
Father Dong cautiously tasted it, and then put the rest in his mouth.
Mmm, it's sweet and rich! You might have finally found a way to preserve our milk!
In the following days, Dong and his father tried different ways of boiling and steaming milk. After many tries, they came up with a smooth custard with the creamy skin formed on top.
It was rich, delicious, and could last much longer than fresh milk.
They called their creation "steamed milk custard" and sold it at the market. Soon people lined up in front of their stall-and they no longer wasted any of their milk. Before long, steamed milk custard became a popular dessert in the Cantonese region, and soon many variations spread all over the world.

# STEAMED MILK CUSTARD
## (鮮奶甜羹)

Steamed milk custard is like a Chinese version of crème brûlée without the crunchy sugar top. It's a soft, gentle custard with a creamy texture. Its velvet mouthfeel comes from a balanced mixture of milk, egg whites, and sugar. This treat has two distinct skins: The first layer forms when the heated milk cools, and the second layer appears when the custard cools. Serve warm or cold with your favorite toppings, such as fresh fruit, nuts, or chocolate chips.

**Makes 4 servings**

1½ cups whole milk
¾ cup light cream
¼ cup granulated sugar
2 egg whites, beaten
1 cup cut fresh fruit, granola, or toasted nuts (optional)

# HOW TO MAKE STEAMED MILK CUSTARD

Set a steamer with water on a stovetop and bring it to a boil over high heat.

In a small saucepan over low heat, combine the milk, light cream, and sugar.

Stir until the sugar dissolves and the mixture is warm to the touch.

In a large mixing bowl, beat the egg whites thoroughly until smooth.

Slowly stir in the milk mixture. Mix well.

Strain the mixture through a fine-mesh sieve, then pour it into four heatproof serving bowls.

Cover each bowl with aluminum foil and place them in the steamer.

Lower the heat to medium and steam the bowls until the milk mixture forms a wobbly consistency of custard, about 10 minutes.

Turn off the heat and leave the custard in the steamer for 10 minutes before removing.

Serve warm or chilled topped with the fruit, granola, or nuts (if using).

To store, seal leftovers in an airtight container and refrigerate for up to 2 days.

# EMPRESS LU ZHI'S BEAUTY SOUP

Following the collapse of the tumultuous Qin dynasty (221–206 BC), a civil officer named Liu Bang established the Han dynasty (202 BC–220 AD). With the help of his wife, Lu Zhi, he became emperor.

Feeling deep gratitude toward his wife, Bang often told her that she was the love of his life and the most beautiful woman in China.

However, as time passed, Liu Bang couldn't resist his attractive young concubines.

Determined to remain the only love in her husband's heart, Empress Lu Zhi visited her husband every morning after his meeting with his ministers in the Forbidden City.

One day, as she walked into the courtyard outside her husband's office, she heard someone playing the flute. She peeked inside the window. Madam Qi, one of the emperor's concubines, performed while her husband stroked her long, shiny hair. Lu Zhi felt as if hundreds of needles were poking her heart.

When the song ended, Emperor Lu clapped loudly.

Qi, you have the shiniest hair in all the court.

What about the empress?

You are **more** beautiful!

HAHAHA

Empress Lu ran back to her bedroom, threw herself down on her bed, and wailed. Her maids surrounded her and asked what was wrong.

When she told them what happened, they suggested how she could make herself more enticing than Madam Qi.

My mother told me that if you soak your hair in fermented rice water or cover it with egg whites, it'll make it shiny.

Tap a needle roller on your scalp. It'll make your hair thicker.

Forget all that! I know a trick. Cover your face with mud from the lotus pond overnight. It'll leave your skin as smooth as silk.

The empress was eager to prove her beauty, so she followed all her maids' advice.

One hot afternoon, the emperor paid Lu Zhi an unexpected visit. When he opened the door, he saw egg whites streaming down her hair and mud caked on her face.

What's going on here? It smells so bad!

All of her maids rushed to comfort the empress in her chambers as she howled.

He'll never love me again!

The youngest maid waited until the others left the room.

Empress, before I left home, my mother shared a family secret with me. She told me never to share it with anyone. But it saddens me to see you in this state, so I will tell you.

She whispered Empress Lu a recipe.

From then on, the young maid cooked a special soup for Empress Lu every day.

Rumors began to spread around the kingdom that Empress Lu's clear complexion, shiny hair, and beautiful smile were due to a unique soup.

Madame Qi offered Lu Zhi's maids money to spill her beauty secret, but to no avail. And before long, Liu Bang turned his attention back to his empress.

After Lu Zhi's death, her young maid opened a restaurant. Women young and old waited outside the door every day long before the shop opened to buy the specialty: "Empress Lu Zhi's beauty soup."

# EMPRESS LU ZHI'S BEAUTY SOUP （皇后美容汤）

In China, watermelon rind is thought to have a cooling effect. During the summer, Nai Nai used it in salads, soups, and stir-fries. The yin-neutral combination of green tea and barley is believed to keep one's skin smooth, firm, and elastic. If you don't have kasha, you can add more oats or substitute another grain like rye. Serve this soup for lunch or as an elegant first course for dinner. While it may not smooth your skin or turn your hair shiny overnight, its taste will brighten your spirits!

## Makes 4 servings

¼ cup rolled oats
¼ cup wheat berries
¼ cup barley
¼ cup brown rice
¼ cup kasha
3 cups watermelon rind, cut into 4 in wide strips
½ cup rock sugar, broken into small pieces
2 green tea bags

# HOW TO MAKE EMPRESS LU ZHI'S BEAUTY SOUP

In a large saucepan, combine the oats, wheat berries, barley, rice, kasha, and watermelon rind.
Add 6 cups of water and bring to a boil.

Cover, turn down the heat to low, and simmer until the liquid has reduced to 4 cups, about 50 minutes.

In a small saucepan, combine the rock sugar, tea bags, and 1 cup of water and bring to a boil.

Turn the heat to medium-low, simmer for 2 minutes, and then remove and discard the tea bags.

Continue to simmer the mixture until the rock sugar has dissolved.

Remove and discard the watermelon rind.

Divide the soup into four bowls and flavor with the sugar and green tea mixture to taste.

Serve warm or at room temperature.

To store, seal leftovers in an airtight container and refrigerate for up to 3 days.

# HOW MANY DIFFERENT REGIONAL CUISINES ARE IN CHINA?

China is home to 56 official ethnic groups.

There are many different styles of Chinese cooking based on ethnic background, local resources, climate, history, and lifestyle.

The eight best-known regional cuisines in China are Cantonese (GuanDong), Sichuan, Jiangsu, Zhejiang, Fujian, Hunan, Anhui, and Shandong. Each has its own cooking methods, custom dishes, and distinctive tastes.

SHANDONG CUISINE

JIANGSU CUISINE

ANHUI CUISINE

ZHEJIANG CUISINE

SICHUAN CUISINE

HUNAN CUISINE

FUJIAN CUISINE

GUANDONG CUISINE

# HOW TO USE CHOPSTICKS

There are several ways to hold and use chopsticks.

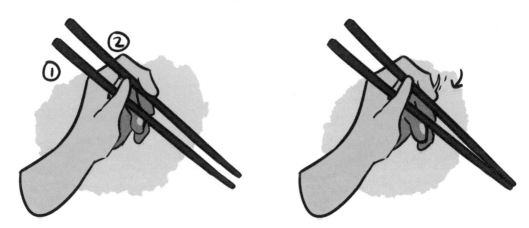

The easiest way is to place the first chopstick between your thumb and index finger. Rest the lower part of the stick on the tip of your ring finger.

Insert the second stick above the first one. Hold it the way you would hold a pencil. Bring the tips of the two sticks together. Keep the first chopstick still while moving the second one with your index and middle fingers.

Beginners can make their own trainer chopsticks. Roll up a piece of paper (like the wrapper for your chopsticks) into a small block. Place the block near the top of the chopsticks. Bind the sticks together just above the block with a rubber band, which will help keep the chopsticks together.

# CHOPSTICKS ETIQUETTE

DO wait to pick up your chopsticks until the eldest person at the table raises theirs to signal the start of the meal.

DON'T use chopsticks to point at anyone. This is like pointing your finger at someone.

DO separate and rub wooden chopsticks together under the table, not above.

DON'T rattle or tap chopsticks against your bowl. It is believed this will break the fortune of the family.

DO rest the tips of your chopsticks on a chopstick stand to the right side of your bowl.

DON'T put chopsticks upright in a bowl of rice. Doing so represents a tombstone.

DO use communal chopsticks to pick up food from sharing dishes.

DON'T use your chopsticks as a skewer for your food. This is seen as rude.

# HOW TO TOAST NUTS

Toasting nuts is all about timing. Toasting time varies depending on the size of the nuts. Larger nuts, such as walnuts, pecans, and almonds, take longer than smaller nuts, such as peanuts and pine nuts.

The key is not to walk away once they start to brown—they can burn quickly! Once cool, store toasted nuts in an airtight container for up to a week.

You can toast nuts in the oven or in a skillet.

| | | | |
|---|---|---|---|
| Preheat the oven to 350°F. | Arrange the nuts in a single layer on a baking sheet. | Place the sheet on the middle rack of the oven and toast until the nuts turn golden brown. | Shake the pan a few times during toasting so the nuts in the middle of the pan toast as quickly as the ones at the edges. Transfer to a plate and cool. |

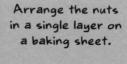

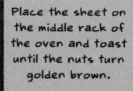

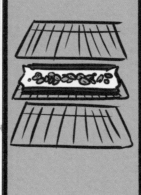

On the stovetop: In a dry skillet over medium-high heat, sauté the nuts for 3 to 5 minutes, stirring frequently, until they start to turn golden brown.

Transfer to a plate and cool.

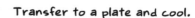

# FINGER TAPPING

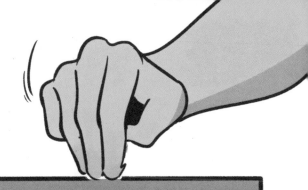

Have you ever seen your Chinese friends tap their fingers on the table when someone fills their teacups and wonder what that's about?

During the Qing dynasty (1644–1911), Emperor Qianlong loved to disguise himself and observe the everyday lives of his people across China. He ordered his accompanying servants not to reveal his identity.

They once stopped at a teahouse in southern China. The emperor's servants took turns pouring tea for everyone at the table. When it was the emperor's turn, his servants stood up to bow to him and to show their gratitude. Emperor Qianlong stopped them.

No, no, sit down!

Just tap three fingers on the table to show your respect.

One finger represents your bowed heads, and the other two represent your prostrated arms. This way, you do not reveal my identity.

The servants were impressed by their emperor's wit.

So wise!

Brilliant!

Genius!

From then on, it became a Chinese custom to show gratitude by tapping two or three fingers when someone fills your teacup as well as a way to not interrupt the conversation!

# TEA-DRINKING ETIQUETTE

The social act of tea drinking has its own rituals and rules.

When pouring tea for guests, don't fill the teacup more than three-quarters of the way.

As a sign of respect, serve elders first.

Always use both hands when presenting others with their teacup.

While everyone should avoid taking large sips when drinking, there are some different rules for men and women.

Men should use their right hand to hold their teacup. The thumb and index finger should be placed on the teacup's rim and the middle finger should support the bottom. For posture, backs should be kept upright with the shoulders relaxed. When not drinking, hands should be laid on the table, open and apart.

Women should follow the same finger placement but with both hands. Some extend their pinky finger for an elegant appearance. Backs and shoulders should also be kept straight and relaxed. When not drinking, hands should also be kept on the table, but unlike men, women should keep their hands together.

Finally, when you are a guest, it is improper to finish the tea in big gulps. You'd feel very guil-tea!

# ETIQUETTE FOR EATING FROM A RICE BOWL

Etiquette? You may think, Just scoop up the rice! Well, that may be easy with a spoon, but those are typically reserved for soups in Chinese dining. Have you tried it with chopsticks?

The biggest challenge while eating rice with chopsticks is how to use the thin sticks to pick up the small grains. Luckily, the Chinese found a solution!

Pick up the rice bowl. Let your thumb rest on the bowl's rim, with your other fingers placed at the bottom for support. While picking up your bowl is considered rude in the West, it's part of Chinese tradition. On the other hand, bending over your food is impolite in China. It's believed that it will squeeze your stomach and prevent healthy digestion.

Next time you are dinning with chopsticks, bring your rice bowl close to your mouth and use the chopsticks as a shovel.

# Equivalents

The equivalents in the following tables have been rounded for convenience.

## Liquid/Dry Measurements

| US | Metric |
|---|---|
| ¼ cup | 60 ml |
| ⅓ cup | 80 ml |
| ½ cup | 120 ml |
| 1 cup | 240 ml |
| 2 cups (1 pt) | 475 ml |
| 4 cups (1 qt; 32 fl oz) | 945 ml |
| 4 qt (1 gal) | 3.8 L |
| | |
| 1 oz (by weight) | 30 g |
| 8 oz (½ lb) | 230 g |
| 16 oz (1 lb) | 455 g |
| 2.5 lb | 1.1 kg |

## Lengths

| US | Metric |
|---|---|
| ⅛ in | 3 mm |
| ¼ in | 6 mm |
| ½ in | 13 mm |
| 1 in | 2.5 cm |

## Oven Temperatures

| Fahrenheit | Celsius |
|---|---|
| 250 | 120 |
| 275 | 135 |
| 300 | 150 |
| 325 | 165 |
| 350 | 180 |
| 375 | 190 |
| 400 | 200 |
| 425 | 220 |
| 450 | 230 |
| 475 | 240 |
| 500 | 260 |

# Acknowledgments

Creating this graphic novel cookbook
has been an incredible journey, and I am
deeply grateful to the amazing team who
helped bring it to life.

First and foremost, my heartfelt thanks to
Vivian Truong for her breathtaking artwork.
Vivian, your stunning illustrations have truly
brought this book to life. Your creativity and
attention to detail have added a unique and
vibrant dimension to the stories and recipes.

To Sarah Billingsley and Alex Galou, my
exceptional editors, thank you for your
unwavering support and insightful guidance.
Your expertise and dedication have been
instrumental in shaping this book into something truly special. I am profoundly grateful
for your hard work and commitment.

A special thanks to Gabriel Cruz for
his meticulous proofreading and keen eye
for detail. Gabriel, your careful review has
ensured the accuracy and clarity
of the text, making the book even
more enjoyable for our readers.

This book is a testament to the collaborative
spirit and dedication of everyone involved.
I am deeply appreciative of each of you
for your contributions. Together, we have
created something wonderful.

Thank you all!

# Index